WILD
LONDON

Also by the authors:

London for Lovers: Romantic Days and Nights Out in the City

WILD
LONDON

Urban Escapes in and around the City

SAM & SOPHIE HODGES

■ SQUARE PEG

1 3 5 7 9 10 8 6 4 2

Square Peg, an imprint of Vintage,
20 Vauxhall Bridge Road,
London SW1V 2SA

Square Peg is part of the Penguin Random House group of companies whose addresses can be found at
global.penguinrandomhouse.com

Text © Sam and Sophie Hodges 2019

Sam and Sophie Hodges have asserted their right to be identified as the authors of this Work
in accordance with the Copyright, Designs and Patents Act 1988

First published by Square Peg in 2019

Penguin.co.uk/vintage

A CIP catalogue record for this book is available from the British Library

ISBN 9781910931622

Designed and typeset by Dan Mogford
Printed and bound in China by C&C Offset Printing Co., Ltd.

Penguin Random House is committed to a sustainable future for our business, our readers and our planet.
This book is made from Forest Stewardship Council® certified paper.

For Wren and Otto

CONTENTS

Introduction   ix

SPRING
Where the Wild Things Are   3
London in Bloom   17
Secret Gardens   29

SUMMER
Get Your Hands Dirty   43
Wet and Wild   53
Cycle Rides   69

AUTUMN

Wildlife Watching 85
A Walk in the Woods 95
Foraging Forays 105
Terrific Trees 121

WINTER

Urban Birding 133
The Great Indoors 147
Festive Spirit 159

Directory and useful addresses 170
Notes 178
Index 179

INTRODUCTION

Forget six counties overhung with smoke,
Forget the snorting steam and piston stroke,
Forget the spreading of the hideous town;
Think rather of the pack-horse on the down,
And dream of London, small, and white, and clean,
The clear Thames bordered by its gardens green.

The Earthly Paradise, William Morris (1834–1896)

London teems as much with nature zealots as it does with nature itself: the quiet hordes that gather at dawn near reservoirs, binoculars at the ready; entire families armed with Tupperware and jam jars, out-craning each other for the fattest of blackberries; steely older women, capped and costumed, lowering themselves, whatever the weather, into the muddy darkness of near-glacial ponds. But through these idiosyncratic rituals, Londoners find a kind of joy: perhaps it is not surprising that the city is full of so many nature lovers when 47 per cent of the capital is green.

The urbanite's longing for nature began around two centuries ago, when our ancestors were wrenched away from life on the land and herded together into cities. Far from losing our passion for nature, industrialisation left city dwellers wanting it more than ever. From beekeeping in Battersea and foraging for mugwort on Walthamstow Marshes, to the 2014 bid to turn London into the first urban national park, the call of the wild has never been louder.

This book is an answer to that call: a celebration of all London has to offer the nature-lover – whether passing through the capital, or a life-long resident. Other than well-trodden trails in the formal parks and gardens, existing tourist guides barely scratch the surface of London's hidden natural wonders.

The book is divided into seasons, as every one of them offers up equally inspiring opportunities to find wildness around the corner. With the exception of sledging, most activities can be enjoyed all year round – overwintering ducks take the place of migratory warblers; wild swimming spots remain destinations, come rain or shine; farm-to-table restaurants are swapped for farm-to-hand in the summer.

London is a city full of people looking but not seeing – distracted by the pressures of the coming day or, more commonly, by the addictive appeal of the phone screen. This book is designed to inspire a more mindful approach, to encourage you to glance skywards for birdlife and trees, and downwards to the roadside verges and railway cuttings, canal towpaths and brownfield sites – what Richard Mabey calls Britain's 'unofficial countryside' – humming with life, waiting to be discovered.

Opposite: Wisteria at The Geffrye Museum. Previous page: Woodberry Wetlands

WHERE THE WILD THINGS ARE

The population of the capital is expected to increase from 8.6 million to 10 million by 2030, inevitably putting increased pressure on roads and housing and raising air pollution levels. London's green spaces are caught in the middle of this – both under threat from developers and yet needed more than ever.

The city's urban farms, ecological parks and nature reserves are protected and expanded due to the concerted efforts of wildlife campaigners and conservationists, who play a huge role in keeping London wild. In recent years, new wildlife sanctuaries have been opened, including **Braeburn Park** in Crayford in 2016, **Walthamstow Wetlands** in 2017 and **Crane Meadows** near Heathrow in 2018. The London Wildlife Trust is even campaigning for a Nature and Wellbeing Act, to enshrine into law the importance of the protection of nature for generations to come.

Opposite: Lee Valley Farm. Previous page: St Dunstan-in-the-East

These green spaces play an increasingly important role in the life of schools, combatting what British childcare expert Tim Gill calls the 'shrinking horizons of childhood.' The Danish concept of the Forest School, which is now featured in over 11,000 sessions each year in the UK, epitomises this new wave of wild education. The Forest School works to the principle that multisensory stimuli – such as the smell of a smoky log fire or the sound of splashing mud – help with memory.

CITY FARMS

We perhaps most associate the Netherlands with canals, windmills, bicycles, Delft Blue pottery and cheese, but in terms of its influence on London, it's by far the children's farm movement that has been the most profound. During the 1960s, community projects of all varieties – youth clubs, tenant associations – were escalating in response to a rising lack of control or ownership of land. But it was Holland that spawned the principle of care farms, or farm-based therapeutic interventions, through interaction with farm animals. London's first city farm, **Kentish Town City Farm**, was established back in 1972 and the movement quickly grew to its current size of 120 farms and nearly 1000 community gardens.

City farms paradoxically give farm animals more attention than they would normally get in a larger farm, but obviously the city farm movement is largely for the benefit of London schoolchildren, providing an educational link between urban and rural life and aiming to improve health and well-being. It has been proven to achieve environmental benefits, encourage healthy eating, exercise and learning, and boost the local economy, volunteerism and community engagement – particularly with young people or those with behavioural problems or learning difficulties. There is even a rise of school farms – there were just sixty in 2006, but now the figure has almost reached a hundred, with another 109 to come.

Kentish Town City Farm remains one of the capital's jewels, with its annual May Day celebrations full of distractions. Tucked away just off Grafton Road, pushing through the farm gates feels like stumbling on a country fête. The pastoral sight of corn dolls, scarecrows, bottle-fed lambs and a ribbon-decked maypole greets the eye. People queue patiently and good-humouredly to have the faces of their young charges painted – if it rains, brollies and macs materialise, but the scene remains unchanged. Teenagers selfie with animals that boast their own Instagram accounts. Dads chomp down on barbecued sausages, waiting to hear news of a return on their raffle tickets. And most importantly, each year's highlight is the annual and much-anticipated bake-off, with judges from the local bakery on hand to sort the wheat from the chaff. The main focus of the UK's oldest city farm is to educate. So there are inevitably countless critters to pat, but there's also a vibrant activity programme that runs six days a week. Kids aged eight and over can help with feeding and mucking out on weekends and holidays.

Lee Valley Park Farms, in the hinterland of greater London, feels a bit more like a theme park than a working farm. The cobbled farmyards are scattered around a large central barn and various outhouses, with Critter Corner at one end and Tortoise Town at the other – everywhere, families gather, children on shoulders, to watch feeding presentations, milking displays and tractor rides. Venturing beyond the farmyard takes visitors into more exotic territory; a meerkat lookout defends an ever-busy mob; opposite, a row of large cages house increasingly dramatic birds of prey, unfazed by their admirers. On the outskirts of the park, there's a racetrack for lambs and pigs, a tobogganing chute for humans surrounded by enclosures of llama, reindeer and miniature zebu. Spring is particularly active for the farm on account of its 'baby boom' – visitors are encouraged to grab a bottle and feed the orphan lambs and piglets.

Perhaps the most dramatically urban is **Mudchute Park and Farm**, with its 32 acres of rolling farmland framed by a backdrop of skyscrapers and tower blocks that make up the financial

district of Canary Wharf and the Isle of Dogs. It was in fact initially created by locals to resist yet more high-rise architecture, and the farm, free to enter, has been a haven of education, aimed at demystifying the origins of food with programmes such as 'from allotment to plate'. Residents include George Clooney (the ram), Danny Dyer (the other ram) and Claus and Columbus (the long-faced llama cousins). There is also an all-weather floodlit riding arena, regular show-jumping competitions held at the Equestrian Centre and the Mudchute Kitchen, which features a great farmer's brunch selection and welcomes pets entering their Pet of the Month competition.

There is even a tiny working farm, **Oasis Waterloo**, crammed into the diminutive strip of land a stone's throw from the South Bank and within sight of the Houses of Parliament. The farm houses animals 'in retreat' from their home on Jamie's Farm in Wiltshire, which uses working farms to engage with disadvantaged children. Interestingly, animals that need more focused care are easier to oversee in the confines of the Waterloo space.

And city farms are not just used to educate the young. With around 850,000 people in Britain suffering from dementia and with loneliness now considered a major public health issue, **Stepney City Farm** has started taking a menagerie of guinea pigs, rabbits, chickens and ferrets to isolated elderly people living in hospitals and nursing homes, to encourage bonding with the animals in a bid to build their self-esteem.

Stepney City Farm hosts a weekly Farmers' Market every Saturday between 10 a.m. and 3 p.m. This is no ordinary set of stalls though – each of the stallholders, from cheesemongers to sausage specialists, knows their stuff intimately and they will be happy to share recipes and advice on their culinary collections. The stalls vary from week to week, but offer a range of organic vegetables, fruit, bread, cheeses, meat, fish, cakes, eggs, olives, preserves, oils and juices.

Mudchute Park and Farm

City farms are now also used to incubate new developments in food production, self-sufficiency and cultivation. The latest innovation in genuine city farming is the literal rise of urban rooftop farms, where both crops and animals are kept in tall, tiered structures that combat space shortages. FARM started in 2011 with their **FARM:shop** in Dalston, which features aquaponics micro fish farming, a high-tech indoor allotment, a micro mushroom farm and a rooftop chicken coop. They are now working towards their vision of a 3,000-square-metre farm on a London rooftop, with food grown in a high-yield, environmentally friendly way.

BUTTERFLY HOUSES

The emergence of a brand-new butterfly from its crisp, brown chrysalis, before it pumps its newly transformed, still-crumpled wings and takes flight, is one of nature's wonders. Each year, Luke Brown, the manager of the butterfly house at the **Natural History Museum**, not only manages the arrival of hundreds of tropical chrysalises into Heathrow, but in some cases, single-handedly assists their delivery, with the aid of a pin. In the wild, the success rate of butterfly 'births' is between 10 and 15 per cent; at the NHM, it's closer to 85 per cent. And that's after Luke and his colleagues have painstakingly glued each chrysalis to a branch in the hatchery.

The museum's annual exhibition, Seasonal Butterflies, features a shallow pool filled with water, salts and minerals for the male butterflies to lap up and present as gifts of seduction to female companions. While unremarkable from the outside, the tent on the museum's east lawn is a window into an extraordinary world of vivid scents and the flashes of blues and yellows and blacks of swallowtails, morphos and birdwings – the latter, one of the largest butterflies in the world, caused Victorian entomologist Alfred Russel Wallace such excitement that he 'felt much more like fainting than I have done when in apprehension of immediate death.'

A large tiger butterfly at the Natural History Museum

In another juxtaposition of the living with the dead, the **Horniman Museum and Gardens** has opened a new Butterfly House, complete with its own puparium; rare butterflies like the Horniman's swallowtail now accompany its famous overstuffed walrus. Unlike the Natural History Museum, this butterfly house is a year-round attraction and features different species depending on what time of year it is.

Whipsnade Zoo, London Zoo's Hertfordshire sister, has also got in on the act with its own chrysalis-shaped butterfly biome. It follows the same immersive route as its competitors, with species such as the Blue Tiger and the Long-Winged Zebra landing on the arms and heads of delighted visitors. The enclosure doubles as a new home for the zoo's West African dwarf crocodiles, for whom the new Butterfly House is their very own luxury hotel.

These initiatives are increasingly vital, as butterfly numbers are in steep decline due to fluctuating weather patterns in recent years. Butterflies are very sensitive to weather and environmental change. Mild winters are harmful due to increased rate of disease and the risk that they emerge from winter hibernation too early. Cold springs limit the ability of butterflies to fly, which prevents them from breeding and laying eggs. Given this sensitivity, the annual **Big Butterfly Count** is a great way to take nature's pulse and identify trends. In July and August, participants are invited to count butterflies for fifteen minutes during bright weather and submit their findings, either online or through the butterfly count app.

ECO-PARKS

Nowadays, we take for granted the opportunity to visit a local ecology park to learn how to pond-dip, bee-keep or simply immerse oneself in the surreal calm of these wild oases. Once again, a leaf was taken out of our Dutch neighbours' book, where heem parks have been well-established as opportunities for inner-city children to interact with nature. In London,

Camley Street Nature Park, King's Cross

the movement started in 1977, when a stretch of derelict land on the south bank of the Thames next to Tower Bridge was temporarily leased to some eco-trailblazers, principally on the basis that it would be cheaper to let them transform it ahead of the Silver Jubilee Walkway than by more conventional landscaping methods. Thus the William Curtis Ecological Park was born, pioneering the notion of a range of habitats in a small area, from meadow to mixed woodland, willow carr to shallow pond. Everything we casually associate with these parks, including groups of young schoolchildren shin-high in murky pondwater, sifting for 'mini-beasts' with nets and buckets, was radical at the time and hugely popular. The William Curtis Ecological Park closed in 1985 to make way for new allotments but its legacy was the redevelopment of zones all along the Thames and of redundant docklands into ecological parks to this day.

The real star attraction of these eco-parks was its most secretive: the near-primordial newt. These crocodilian creatures are surprisingly common in London, especially in and around garden ponds. The smooth is the most widespread, from Willesden to Tottenham. During breeding season, between late March and late May, a torch beam cast into the depths of a pond at night will reveal the wavy wrinkled crest or bright red or yellow belly of the male in his courtship plumage. The palmate, whose best distinguishing features are his dark webbed hind feet, is more at home in the acid pools of Surrey heathland or Epping Forest, so less likely to be observed. The great crested is the fussiest of the three, turning its warted nose up at garden ponds in favour of larger, deeper bodies of water. Amphibian, the newt's class of vertebrate, literally means 'both sides of life'. The newt divides both sides quite neatly according to the time of year – its only aquatic phase, in spring, is for the purpose of mating and egg-laying, the rest of the year is dedicated to a more terrestrial routine. The great crested has even been found up to half a kilometre from its birth pond. In summer, they go deeper and darker, sometimes even entering a hibernation-like state to escape the dry heat and conserve water – only returning to the water in early spring again.

Frogs, a close relative, follow a more traditional winter hibernation before reawakening, like nature's very own Sleeping Beauty, in March. The **Greenwich Peninsula Ecology Park** hosts an annual Frog Day to celebrate, with frogspawn encounters, frog mask-making and the specially designed 'What Does the Frog Say?' prize trail. The park is another example of heavy industry transformed into natural wonder – in this case, 121 hectares of neglected land, once a huge shipbuilding yard and gas and chemical works. Explorers use wooden decked bridges to cross lily-covered canals, brushing up against 8-foot reed beds, from which the sounds of warblers and wrens can be heard. There are even two hotels in the park now … for insects. Along with a willow tunnel and timber team swing, they make up the eco-playpark for children, using natural and reclaimed materials such as York stone and bark mulch.

Yet another jewel in the civic crown that is the King's Cross redevelopment is **Camley Street Nature Park**, tucked away between Regent's Canal towpath and the triumphant Victorian Gothic spires of the 'cathedral of railways', St Pancras International. Giant, wrought-iron gates swing open off the unassuming Camley Street into a 2-acre haven in the heart of one of London's most densely populated areas. The park is another example of London's recent track record in successfully converting industrial sites into the urban wild; originally it was used to store coal dropped to service the trains in and out of King's Cross railway station. The London Wildlife Trust has squeezed every possible habitat out of this boutique reserve, from a fernery in the woods to a reed bed, both a home for warblers and a purification system for the water that trickles past. An otherwise incongruous pile of logs stakes its claim as a home for stag beetles beside a wildflower meadow doing the same in summer for bees and butterflies.

Camley's finest attractions are both on the canal itself, a perfect collision of the natural and the man-made. Through the copses of very English-sounding apple trees ('Margaret', 'Greensleeves' and 'Egremont Russet'), three giant rusting arrow heads seem to loom out of the ground. On closer inspection these are the sculpted edges of the first attraction, a floating

platform, Viewpoint, created by young Finnish architects recalling their rocky islands off the Nordic coastline. Designed as a place of sanctuary, this islet offers a new perspective of kingfishers and other canal life. At the other end of the park is moored the second, another bankside novelty – a 1940s canal dredger that started its life collecting silt and rubbish from the canal bed and which has now been turned into a floating forest garden. Using the unique layering of forest gardening, the oldest agro-horticultural style in use, this small barge manages to hold over a hundred different types of plant, all in some form edible. Perhaps the most significant is the elm tree, which is staging a comeback; once prolific in and around London, a great many were destroyed by Dutch elm disease in the 1970s.

Further north, in the shadows of Arsenal Football Club's Emirates Stadium and framed on one side by railway tracks, cow parsley, wild carrot, kidney vetch and other wild flowers accent a long meadow that snakes into **Gillespie Park**, another coal store turned nature reserve. To the east of the sidings, H. C. 'Inky' Stevens opened an ink factory, which kept producing until the 1960s. In the years following, the area was disputed – new council homes, parking spaces for the football club, private development. A development deal was struck in 1992, which included the building of an ecology centre and the protection of Islington's only orchid, a common spotted orchid. It is now home to hundreds of flowering plants, birds, butterflies and water creatures, as well as a rare lichen – *Peltigera didactyla*. The park is compact and an easy stroll through meadow and wetland and wood.

Bee-keeping at Gillespie Park

LONDON IN BLOOM

Few things rival the giddy sense of hope and explosion of new life as spring in Britain. Thawing ground is broken by small green spikes, pushing past leaf litter, releasing scents which fill the air optimistically. Flowers in particular have captivated writers over the years; perhaps it's their transience and fragility, coupled with the fact that they herald a new era of light and warmth, that give them an almost sacred significance. In *Hamlet*, Shakespeare describes the violet as 'in the youth of primy nature, / Forward, not permanent, sweet, not lasting, / The perfume and suppliance of a minute.'

BLUEBELLS

The bluebell, also known as wild hyacinth, wood bell, bell bottle, cuckoo's boots, witches' thimbles, or lady's nightcap, is the country's favourite flower. It is what the robin is for birds

Bluebells in bloom, Wanstead Park

and the oak is for trees – a national treasure, synonymous with hope and promise. Unique to the western shores of the Eurasian landmass, where it is mild and wet, these purple bells transform the ancient woodland that they populate by covering the ground as far as the eye can see.

A poetic muse for the Romantic poets in particular, the bluebell has been immortalised by Keats, who described it as the 'Sapphire queen of the mid-May', by Tennyson, who compared a field of bluebells to 'the blue sky, breaking up through the earth', and Gerard Manley Hopkins who went even further: 'in falls of sky-colour washing the brows and slacks of the ground with vein-blue.'

The true bluebell is under threat from its Spanish cousin, distinguishable by the colour of the slim pollen fingers that peek out from within its bell. Native species have white-cream-coloured pollen, while the Armada's is blue; the latter also possesses less of the classic droop that gives our famous wildflower its false modest hunch.

The bluebell can be found the length and breadth of the country, from Cape Wrath at the northern tip of Scotland to the Isles of Scilly, England's southernmost frontier. Similarly, London's four corners turn blue every May.

In the east of the city, Chalet Wood of **Wanstead Park** is a prime spot, near the Temple. Thousands of bluebells erupt each year, although they can fall prey to their own popularity; with no clearly defined pathways, the draw to photograph from within the colony can be too strong for some visitors to resist. Walking among the flowers often compacts the ground and makes it harder for the tender stems to break through.

Once called the Great Ditch Wood, **Gutteridge Wood** in Hillingdon is an ancient oak and hazel coppice woodland that bursts to life each year, not just with bluebells, but with birdlife – kingfisher, great spotted and green woodpecker and nuthatch can all be seen flying from tree to tree while above them soar or hover kestrel, hobby, buzzard and red kite. The northernmost border of the wood features a wildflower meadow, a stunning counterpoint to the oak and hazel of the wood.

Known as the lungs of south London for its oasis of oxygen-producing foliage amid an urban jungle of vehicles and buildings, **Oxleas Wood**, which dates back to the end of the last Ice Age, was designated a Site of Scientific Interest because of the many and often rare species of trees and insects that can be found there. An annual bluebell walk starts at the historic **Severndroog Castle** on Shooter's Hill and takes in a plethora of wild flowers, including stitchwort, lady's smock, wood sorrel, wild garlic and wood anemones, as well as bluebells.

Come spring, **Osterley Park** in south-west London is awash with purple flowers. The Long Walk and the Great Meadow are full of native English bluebells, with their distinctive sweet smell, while the walls of the Tudor mansion itself groan under the weight of impressively vast wisteria plants.

CAMELLIAS

Camellias have, like no other flower, bloomed in and out of fashion over the last two centuries. The flower's English presence is largely down to the 6th Duke of Devonshire, a passionate horticulturalist who built a palatial new conservatory on the grounds of **Chiswick House** in 1813 – one of the earliest and most impressive of its kind. Initially this was for vines, peaches and figs, but as a certain Alfred Chandler began importing camellias from China, sometimes enduring arduous and stormy six-month crossings, the conservatory developed a new muse. The girth of some existing trees, 'Chandleri', 'Rubra Plena', 'Variegata', 'Imbricata', 'Alba Plena', 'Pompone', suggests they could date from the 1820s.

However, despite this promising start, the conservatory was difficult to maintain – by 1932, it was falling down and had to be rebuilt. It was repaired following damage during the Second World War, and then again in 1983. And all the while, these pink and red multi-petalled balls of colour persisted. In fact, it transpired that the damage to the conservatory might have been their lifeline – contrary to early nineteenth-century thinking, which assumed incorrectly that they should be cultivated in hothouses, the broken windows appealed to their hardiness, a quality which now sees them planted outside. And so the conservatory pottered on – overgrown, unloved, its inhabitants doggedly clinging to life – until in 1994 a newcomer to Chiswick House, volunteer Jane Callander, overcame her nerves and stood up at the international Camellia Society to alert the top dogs. Over the coming weeks and months, they went to battle with sooty mould and years of neglect, and coaxed the population of Chinese immigrants back to life. Now, each spring, the thirty-three heritage camellias light up the 300-foot glasshouse, heralding the annual **Camellia Show** in Chiswick House and Gardens.

A curious anomaly of the camellia is that despite its beauty and the fact that its leaves are used for tea and its seeds for sweet seasoning and cooking oil, the camellia has no fragrance. Strangely, the range of perfume collections named after the camellia, which offer, for example, 'fragrant camellias on a pedestal, subtly warmed with elemi resins' or 'a very feminine composition of red-petalled flower', are all based on 'fantasy notes' built around the concept of the camellia's beauty rather than any actual scent, a sort of meta-fragrance that gives the illusion of a natural source.

Windsor Great Park just outside London is another prime spot for camellias. In particular, its Valley Gardens are 250 acres of rolling valleys planted with an internationally acclaimed collection of blooms and exotic shrubs, which have been continually planted since the middle of the eighteenth century.

CROCUSES

Spangling the turf, like hundreds of two-tone sweets thrown across the lawn, the crocus is the spring flower that most fully lives up to the idea of 'carpeting' the grass with its blooms. And the effect can seem to happen overnight; their stems silently spear the grass, unnoticed, until they fling open their petals to greet the sun.

Crocuses are the gardener's harbinger of spring; in fact, even the financial community sometimes refers to companies or economic sectors that rise early after an economic downturn as 'crocuses', in reference to the flower's ability to thrive in the late winter or early spring. Along with daffodils, snowdrops and cyclamen, crocuses are good candidates for naturalising – the technique of scattering bulbs and allowing them to seed where they land and spread wherever they choose. *C. tomassinianus* is one of the few crocuses to naturalise readily in the UK – 'Ruby Giant' is violet-mauve and 'Whitewell Purple' has a mauve exterior and pale interior. The common Dutch crocus hybrids are less straight and rather more blowsy, but have great names – 'Remembrance' (silvery-purple), 'Vanguard' (two-tone purple and silvery-lilac), 'Snowstorm' (white), 'Jeanne d'Arc' (white with purple base).

Crocuses in Clissold Park

The word 'crocus' ultimately traces back to the Sanskrit *kunkumam*, 'saffron', and the spice itself comes from the stigmas of *Crocus sativus*, or saffron crocus, an autumn-blooming species. In the last decade, saffron has returned to the fields of England for the first time in two hundred years – only a stone's throw from the town of Saffron Walden, the original Tudor home of saffron harvesting. English saffron was reputed to be the best in the world, with a sweet and honey-like taste. But each flower has to be hand-picked at just the right moment and then dissected in order to remove the three red stigmas from each one, and on account of this painstaking process, saffron growing eventually died out in Britain – it couldn't compete with the cheap imports from Iran and Kashmir. But the home-grown business has taken off again, and local saffron is now on the shelves at Fortnum & Mason and Partridges.

Both **Cannizaro Park** in Wimbledon and the lawns near Palm House at **Kew Gardens** are two of the most spectacular crocus carpets – a purple-white haze that trembles delicately in the breeze, each plant craning upwards, as if to outdo the next.

AZALEAS AND RHODODENDRONS

There has been considerable confusion over the years about the differences between the azalea and the rhododendron. The confusion began with the famous scientist Linnaeus, who established the genus Rhododendron in 1753. His naming established 'Azalea' as a separate genus but it was soon pointed out that azalea plants should be considered a subset of the Rhododendron genus instead, so the rule of thumb is now that all azaleas are Rhododendrons (with a capital letter) but there are just plain rhododendrons that are also fellow members of the genus. Generally speaking, rhododendrons are larger shrubs than azalea plants and have larger leaves. Also, azalea flowers have five stamens while rhododendrons have ten.

Azaleas at Kenwood House

The most impressive display of both can be seen in late April and early May at the **Isabella Plantation**, a 42-acre woodland garden set within a Victorian woodland plantation in **Richmond Park**. Back in the seventeenth century, the area was known as The Sleyt, the name used for boggy ground or open spaces between woods and riverbanks – so, given its well-kept appearance nowadays, there is a distinct sense of this liminal space having been reclaimed for an altogether more glorious purpose. Its name has been the source of debate – some assume Isabella was the wife or daughter of a member of staff, others believe it to be a corruption of the word 'isabel', used to mean dingy or greyish yellow – the colour of the soil. Dingy as it may be, the soil has been the giver of life to a jaw-dropping display of evergreen azaleas that line the plantation's ponds and streams, against the backdrop of a wooden valley; the flowers are mirrored in the still waters, doubling the hypnotic effect of pinks, purples, oranges, whites and greens.

A recent £1.6-million restoration has made the whole experience a major draw – with the newly silted ponds and replanted rhododendrons perfecting the picture, and resurfaced paths for wheelchairs improving access to it. Among the spring highlights are the tall 'Loderi King George' hybrid rhododendrons, with their large, soft and sweetly fragrant pink flowers, and the *R. williamsianum*'s elegant bronze shoots, lily-shaped leaves and bell-shaped, mottled pink flowers.

At the other end of London, the display at **Kenwood House** in May is equally impressive. Like a jostling family portrait, the different-coloured hybrids, *R. catawbiense*, *R. ponticum* and *R. caucasicum*, bunch at various heights, in glorious clumps of orange, lilac and red. The tallest plants tower overhead, such that the intrepid visitor can be enveloped by them and literally immerse themselves in the riot of colour and scent.

WILDFLOWER MEADOWS

Since the 1930s, over 97 per cent of the UK's wildflower meadows have disappeared – the equivalent to a staggering 7.5 million acres. This loss, unrivalled within the history of nature conservation, began in earnest during the Second World War, when grasslands were ploughed to grow cereals. Previously, traditional farming practices would ensure that meadows for hay followed an annual cycle of growing; farmers took grazing animals off the meadows in early spring so the grass and herbs could flower and grow tall before being harvested in July as hay for the farm animals' winter fodder. As tractors replaced farm horses, the demand for hay lessened and it was ultimately then replaced altogether by silage as a form of animal feed.

Wildflower meadows are hugely important hotspots for biodiversity. With as many as 150 species in one spot, from bright golden buttercups to the maroons and purples of clover, knapweed and spotted orchids, they support a plethora of insects, from bees and beetles to grasshoppers and butterflies, which form the basis of a multi-layered food pyramid. Meadows also lower the risk of flooding and air pollution by absorbing both rain water and carbon dioxide, so the ripple effect of reducing 1.7 million hectares to a pitiful current-day 15,000 hectares, scattered like a last wave of resistance fighters in far-flung corners of the country, is barely imaginable. But just as significant as their eco-credentials is the experience of sitting within a wildflower meadow, immersing oneself in the mindful haven of birdsong, insect buzz and wildflower colour.

In spite of the loss of wildflower meadows across the UK, it is possible to recreate them on an individual basis, from a small patch of urban garden to larger tracts of land. There are two types of meadow: a perennial meadow and an annual meadow. Perennial meadows are made up of grasses, knapweed, orchids, cowslips, vetches and agrimony, and will grow back every year if managed correctly. It's a self-perpetuating cycle, which depends on keeping the grasses under control so that they don't stifle the plants – this can be done either through ensuring the garden has soil that is low in fertility or by planting the likes of yellow rattle,

which preys on grass. This method is labour-intensive – the adage goes 'one year's seeding means seven years' weeding'. On the other hand, the annual meadow embraces the more elegant 'weeds' of wheat and barley. This method follows the patterns of the arable field of old – every year, the loosening and tilling of ground prepares it for the 'weeds' that thrive in the tilth. This method allows for more control and with it, the capacity for flowering longevity.

Professors Nigel Dunnett and James Hitchmough, who were behind the design of the **Olympic Park**, perfected this approach over two years of trial runs, even giving their meadows a 'Chelsea chop' (a heavy prune in late May, the time of the annual Chelsea Flower Show, designed to control flowering season) to ensure that everything was in flower for the Olympics, rather than in May and June. Their meadow featured thousands of marigolds, tickseed and corn – marigold hybrids to create the 'ribbon of Olympic gold' around the stadium. The designers hoped that the park would become a blueprint for how green spaces in cities should be managed in the future – swapping formal

Wildflower meadow at the Olympic Park, Stratford

summer bedding for wild meadows. Like the wild prairies themselves, the idea is spreading. The Coronation Meadows project, started to celebrate the sixtieth anniversary of the Queen's coronation, has planted 1000 acres of new wildflower meadows in London's Royal Parks, using the traditional method of horse and harrow to 'scratch' the ground before planting. Other recent initiatives include the Save our Magnificent Meadows partnership and even the first ever National Meadows Day on 4 July 2015.

The planting of wildflower meadows has become increasingly popular in recent years, as the fashion has shifted away from the formal planting styles associated with the Royal Parks. Hyde Park itself now has many wildflower beds, including the **Bumblebee Border** on West Carriage Drive, planted specifically to attract bumblebees, and sheep have even been introduced into Green Park for the first time since the 1930s as part of Prince Charles's efforts to bring wildflower meadows back to London. It is hoped that this traditional method of using grazing sheep will tame the dominant plants in the meadow and allow the wildflowers to populate and flourish. A lesser-known gem is the **Queen Elizabeth Hall Roof Garden** atop the Southbank Centre, open from mid April to the end of September, whose wildflowers and vegetable patches are maintained by a group of volunteers who have all experienced homelessness, mental health or substance-abuse problems. This peaceful spot, particularly good for a weekday brunch, has a café and panoramic views across the Thames.

SECRET GARDENS

The famous nineteenth-century art critic John Ruskin said, 'a measure of a city's greatness is to be found in the quality of its public spaces, its parks and squares'. Each June, London's **Open Gardens Squares Weekend** opens up over two hundred secret gardens that are otherwise closed to the public eye. Past unveilings have included the garden at **10 Downing Street**, the minimalist modern garden at Highbury where once Arsenal footballers played their weekly matches and the **Master's Garden** within the Temple Complex.

However, for some, the city needs to go further to open up its green spaces to the public. Ironically, while park-keepers struggle to provide beautiful green spaces for the city's residents, tourists and commuters (**Green Park** welcomes a million people a month in the summer), Buckingham Palace Gardens, the largest private green space in central London, remains closed to the public. Forbidding walls prevent even a view of the gardens' trees and bushes. Given that the incumbent royals are always away in August and September, some

King Henry's Walk Garden, Islington

have argued that they should follow in the tradition of their forebears – King Charles II began by opening St James's to the public in the 1660s, while Green Park and Regent's Park were opened in 1826 and 1845 respectively.

Christopher Wren once said, 'Architecture aims at Eternity.' Many of his London churches were destroyed during the Blitz, but **St Dunstan-in-the-East**, originally built in Saxon times, has forged its own sort of eternity. Located halfway between the Tower of London and London Bridge, it was significantly damaged during the Great Fire, along with eighty-seven other London churches, but it was rebuilt and even topped with a new steeple designed by London's star architect. However, during the Blitz of autumn 1940 – often described as the Second Great Fire – in which London saw sixty consecutive nights of bombing and the flattening of over a million homes, a direct hit destroyed all of St Dunstan but its north and south walls and Wren's steeple.

Now, the rigorous tendrils of figs, palms, banana plants and grape vines wind their way through and around tall, gothic windows, the glass long since gone – like a Cambodian temple in London's heart. With an abundance of natural light, which Wren would have approved of, the church has become a monument to natural beauty, its towering height echoed by the trees that have grown, unfettered, over the last fifty years. In 1970, the space was restored as a public garden and today hosts the busy lunchtimes of local workers from the nearby financial district. Like their penitential forefathers, they sit and reflect on the various benches, scattered among the ruins. The juxtaposition of light, traceried windows and plants even became the inspiration for an award-winning wallpaper print design, catapulting its emerging designer with an interest in lost architecture into the professional world. St Dunstan-in-the-East has also inspired a wider plan by the Corporation of London to transform former graveyards into places of beauty open to all, partly in response to the fact that the City's working population is expected to rise from 401,000 to 428,000 by 2026.

London's cemeteries feature some of the most striking examples of natural takeovers. **Abney Park**, in Stoke Newington, boasts the first arboretum to have been combined with a cemetery in all of Europe, with around 2,500 trees and bushes. Now gravestone and branch seem to spill out of each other, overlooked by the Dissenting Gothic chapel created for all non-denominational burials, another European first. More recently, the cemetery has been the focus of restoration projects – the Abney Wildflower Project was given £2,000 by Tesco Bags of Help to buy seeds, bulbs and the necessary tools to plant various wildflower meadows across the cemetery; there are also efforts to significantly restore the chapel and revamp the park so that it can host concerts, theatre productions and craft workshops.

It is always intriguing to take one of London's many built-up neighbourhoods and wind back history's clock to uncover a more open and natural past. Rumour has it that King Henry VIII owned a few homes in Newington Green, in north-east London, and liked to stroll from the corner of the green down to a turnpike by the Ball's Pond. One might imagine that the monarch was looking to get some country air away from the travails of mass uxoricide, church sacking and the urban sprawl of Westminster. Now, five hundred years later, Islington has a reputation for being the least green borough in London, in terms of green space per head. And yet King Henry's Walk is home to one of London's best-kept natural secrets, despite having won multiple community garden awards since opening in 2007. In the late nineteenth century, the site now known as **King Henry's Walk Garden** was a timber yard, owed by a firm that described its business as 'contractors for gas, water and public works, well sinkers and borers', a world of industry far removed from its current purpose. Throughout the twentieth century, it fell in and out of use – at one time it was a rose garden created by Islington Council, at another, its discreet environs made it the perfect rendezvous for local prostitutes and drug dealers.

Now, the site features a series of small community allotments assigned to local residents. A pathway to one side of a car park leads through a large metal gate, adorned from top to

bottom in metal leaves, themselves a symbol of the urban wild to be found beyond. The garden itself is a collection of allotments on raised beds; one intriguingly has a hand-written sign with a downward-pointing arrow and the promise of an 'underground bunker' below. There's a wooden bridge, which divides a lily-pad-covered pond, and the back walls of a row of terraced houses stretch one entire side of the garden, on which fruit trees are trained to the walls in the Vass technique. Inside the garden, another gate leads onto **Docwra's Wood**, a self-seeded woodland of mainly sycamore and ash growing on the site of an old factory site. The woodland follows a circular path through silver birch and whitebeam, past a hibernaculum, bug hotels and beehives, and ending at a bench made from rough-hewn logs under a large hornbeam. The final corner of the woodland has been cordoned off with a large man-made thicket of intertwining branches, created to prevent humans from disturbing the wildlife that lives there. In the activity hut and throughout the site, the volunteer-run garden conducts year-round activities, from beekeeping courses to natural shampoo-

Centre for Wildlife Gardening, Peckham

making, storytelling to cold smoking. The garden is particularly engaged with its local Turkish and Kurdish community, who host an annual barbecue, and one year, the garden even grew into the surrounding streets as part of the Chelsea Fringe initiative, installing nine pop-up vegetable gardens on street corners in Mildmay.

In Peckham, south-east London, another secret garden lurks behind two giant, ornately decorated wrought-iron gates. Silhouetted flowers, leaves and birds (there's even one feeding its young if you look closely) reminiscent of Rob Ryan's paper cuttings promise something altogether more delightful than the Victorian terraced housing on either side. Colourful graffiti murals line the alleyway, which finally opens onto the **Centre for Wildlife Gardening**, another example of imaginative city planning, this time orchestrated by the Wildlife Trust in the late 1980s. A resourceful use of space unveils hidden nooks and surprising features on either side of a low ramped bridge leading up to the wooden eco-building visitors centre, complete with classroom and lots of advice and information for gardeners. To the left, sunflowers loom from among a collection of raised, timber-framed beds crowded with lavender, poppies and a forest of herbs. Elsewhere, metal and bamboo wigwams act as staking frames, and wooden greenhouses protect young plants and seedlings in the lead-up to springtime. To the right of the ramp, a wood-chipped pathway, marked with handcrafted fences, meanders through a woodland copse, past shallow ponds and even a so-called multi-storey mini-beast mansion, made up of a tower of wooden pallets stuffed with logs, tubers, empty snail shells, plant pots and general tunnel-making paraphernalia, which welcomes hibernating lacewings and ladybirds and even breeding bees. Round one corner, a semicircle of log seats nestles beneath a regal arbor of intertwining tree trunks, inviting visitors to sit and enjoy the garden's stillness.

The Geffrye Museum Garden is all about historical accuracy, diligently recreating planting choices from each of the last four centuries. The front gardens, with their vast formal lawns and stately centenarian plane trees leading to the chapel, are eye-catching – and consequently filled with office workers from nearby Kingsland Road during weekday lunchtimes. But they are by no means the main event. The first of the back gardens is walled away behind a black wooden door, adding to the sense of a secret past; inside is a traditionally arranged herb garden, in four quadrants, centred around a large bronze sculpture by Kate Malone. Each wall is hugged by a pergola-covered bench, from which the garden's 170 different herbs can be quietly contemplated, from the bee-seducing golden rod and sage to the dangerous monkshood, also known as wolf's bane – its common name is derived from the Greek *lycoctonum*, possibly indicating its use in the poisoning of arrows or baits to kills wolves. The Overground line trains passing through nearby Hoxton station glide overhead, juxtaposing the ancient natural with the modern mechanical, while also ensuring that all passing travellers become potential visitors, their curiosity piqued by the sights below.

Beyond the herb garden lie further historic gardens; blueprints, maps, garden plans and diaries were amassed and pored over in their planning, to ensure the different centuries were reflected accurately. The first garden is a knot garden – a Renaissance garden of very formal design, with a square frame and the edges of each line made from grey-leaved *Santolina chamaecyparissus* and wall germander. It has been said that the symmetrical formality of this Elizabethan garden design is an elegant analogy for the patterns of repetition and variation in rhetorically ornamented speech. In Shakespeare's *Love's Labour's Lost*, one of his most verbally elaborate comedies, Ferdinand, the king of Navarre, uses it as a reference point for 'that obscene and preposterous event, that draweth from my snow-white pen the ebon-coloured ink, which here thou viewest, beholdest, surveyest, or seest; but to the place where; it standeth north-north-east and by east from the west corner of thy curious-knotted garden.'

As the Georgians take over, the garden starts to change in role, becoming an 'outside room', where one would entertain or relax. Tidiness and simplicity was everything – in contrast to this century's custom of covering every last patch of bare earth. Evergreen shrubs such as box, holly and laurel, which could be neatly clipped into shapes, became popular along

with a few seasonal specimens such as the dense mats and round white heads of candytuft. A special feature in this garden is the auricula theatre designed to show off blossoming flowers on shelves that stagger the height and depth of display.

The mid nineteenth-century garden ventures further into domesticated gardening, reflecting the Victorians' enthusiasm for densely planted carpet bedding. The design, based on archive photos of an actual Hackney garden, features a small but perfectly formed greenhouse, shrubbery and an annual bedding display with its own pelargonium pyramid, a somewhat absurd Victorian innovation where zonal geraniums are grown into a tall cone-shaped hedge. Finally, the Edwardian cottage garden demonstrates a clear rejection of the Victorians' more formal taste. In May, the air is filled with the perfume of the blowsy purple wisteria that hangs from the pergola and in June, the climbing rose that faces it blooms for visitors and nesting blue tits alike.

The 1970s was a magical time for Covent Garden. With the flower market moving out to Nine Elms and a change in planning legislation meaning that blue-collar trades made way for office space, the area became quieter, with more activities for local families. Seven community gardens were developed on vacant sites. Nowadays, only the **Phoenix Garden**, created on the site of a former car park, remains. Described on its Twitter page as 'where the West End's frogs live', the park is also a haven for birds right in the heart of London's best-known area; blue and great tit, wren, robin, blackbird, greenfinch, woodpecker, kestrel and sparrowhawk. On the corner of the site next to St Giles-in-the-Fields church, the Phoenix Garden Trust commissioned a new building as the entrance into the garden. The structure features a large arched doorway that is framed by brick walls designed to replicate the garden wall aesthetic and matching the existing low walls that line the garden – a 'metaphor for ideas of enclosure, secrecy and boundaries'. At the far end of the building, a full-width glazed wall swings open through multiple doors into the garden, blurring the line between outdoor and indoors. Finally, the roof of the new building has added 90 square metres of green space to the garden. The themes of sustainability encapsulated in the design continue an existing motif; the dry-stone walls in the garden are built from reclaimed bomb rubble from deep below the garden – the site was directly bombed in 1940.

The origins of many of London's gardens share a common thread – the understanding that immersion in natural beauty can offer escape from the suffocating atmosphere of urban sprawl. Long before the concepts of well-being and mindfulness were as widely acknowledged as they are today, history shows social reformers and pioneers time and time again fighting for green space on behalf of community health. Nineteenth-century Bankside was as grim and squalid as London has ever been, and from this industrial apocalypse Octavia Hill, the co-founder of the National Trust, established a garden designed to be 'an open air sitting room for the tired inhabitants of Southwark.' Laid out on the site of a derelict paper factory, **Red Cross Garden** uses meandering paths to create the illusion of space and an ornamental pond with yellow irises, a bridge and fountain to offer visitors a place to sit and contemplate. Hill also designed a covered play area for children and a walkway for viewing the garden, and she commissioned colourful mosaics to bring art to the working poor. Nowadays, only The Sower remains – a incitement to all city dwellers to return to the soil. In April, the garden is crammed with red tulips in honour of the Red Cross and in May, local children dance around a maypole to herald the coming spring.

Another pleasing theme in this tour of London's secret gardens is the conversion of devastation to creation, of death to new life, a sort of pastoral resurrection project. On Bonnington Square, in south London, a stretch of seven terraced houses were destroyed by a bombing raid during the Second World War. The wound had been left untended for decades, surrounded by a chain-link fence. A token effort by the council in the 1970s saw a slide and swing erected, but they soon fell into dilapidation. A lone walnut tree fought an army of bindweed and buddleia. Finally, in 1990, when the site attracted the curiosity of developers, a local resident spoke to the council about turning it into a community garden, and once

this was approved, the community sprang into action. Raised beds were spread over the basements of the old houses and by way of sculptural interest, a giant slip wheel was rescued from a nearby marble factory where it was once used to cut marble.

Landscape designer and regular gardening columnist Dan Pearson collaborated with fellow resident and New Zealand garden designer James Frazer, so together the planting scheme and the **Bonnington Square Pleasure Gardens** were born. The name is a throwback to the Vauxhall Pleasure Gardens, a phenomenon of the eighteenth and early nineteenth centuries, where commercial gardens were created as privately run sites of entertainment. Throughout the summer months, the gardens would open from early evening; paying visitors were entertained with music and refreshments, while artificial park lights, an attraction in themselves, ensured the evenings were long and magical.

Bonnington Square's version is an homage to the sensory dream-world that Vauxhall represented, both in its creation and its use, and it changed the life on the square. The following year, the Paradise Project extended the vision yet further, greening the streets around the square. Climbers colonised walls, Judas trees lined the pavements, roof gardens rippled outwards in every direction and, most importantly, a new generation of gardeners was inspired.

According to urban myth, the iron wheel from the marble factory turns once a year, mining crystal clear champagne from the worlds below. One midnight, a fishing boat, floating on a sea of wisteria above the pergola, set sail and was never seen again.

Bonnington Square

SUMMER

GET YOUR HANDS DIRTY

It is particularly noticeable that Londoners like to get naked at the first glimmer of summer's arrival, laying down sunbathing towels and picnicking rugs over every available patch of grass in the city's parks. But this summer love of the outdoors does not just extend to burning backs and arms to a reddish crisp or wheeling the BBQ out of its winter hibernation. The summer heralds the season of doing – from exercising outdoors with military-themed bootcamps, to growing fruit and vegetables in allotments, or even nature activism in the back garden.

PICK-YOUR-OWN
London is groaning with organic farmers' markets – **Brixton Farmers' Market**, **Alexandra Palace**, **Balham**, **Marylebone**, **Brockley**, **Walthamstow**, **Pimlico Road**, **Parliament Hill** and many others, part of the increasingly fashionable drive to bring food from farm to table as directly as possible.

Opposite: Frensham Great Pond. Previous page: Copas Farm

During the summer months, when the weather's nice, it's much more fun – for adults and children alike – to go straight to the source. The rural calm of the pick-your-own farm is quite a contrast to the hustle and bustle of the urban farmers' market, where locals jostle for overpriced organic produce. The capital is surrounded by fertile farmland, which means a selection of quiet and picturesque farms in the near vicinity. Only a short drive away, a day's modest exertion can result not only in bags of fresh fruit and veg, but also in the satisfaction of knowing exactly where they came from.

Copas Farm, Iver

An understated but charming roadside pick-your-own experience. Berries seem to be the headliner here – strawberries and raspberries for much of the summer, blackcurrants and cherries more sporadically. For the most part, it's families that drift up and down the chest-high berry beds – later in the day, after the best of the crop has gone, a more eagle-eyed picking technique is required. Around lunchtime, the apple orchards form shady spots for a fruit-filled picnic, with some visitors unloading blankets and pre-packed hampers. There are also ground-level vegetables to be plucked – the yellow-flowered courgette is particularly satisfying to snap off.

Parkside Farm, Enfield

The impressive 50 acres of Parkfield Farm, just on the outskirts of Enfield in north London, picked up the FARMA Pick-Your-Own of the Year Award in 2015, on account of its appetite for experimentation, giving rise to some twenty different crops. One of their key features is 'table-top' strawberries to avoid having to bend down. Nearby, the **Trent Country Park** offers a mosaic of habitats and rambling opportunities, from woodlands to lakes – and so much wildlife that it even has its own rescue and ambulance service within the park.

Garsons Farm, Esher

If you're after pick-your-own on an epic scale, Garsons is the largest in the UK – although for most of its 150-year existence, its purpose was to supply London's Borough Market rather than providing access directly to its fields. Over the course of its long history, farming methods have changed radically to feed the appetite of over 100,000 pickers each summer. The scale of the operation means that they are able to experiment with food trends – in recent years, squash, beetroot, spinach and even kohlrabi have become available for picking. In the past, the farm would trade spent vegetable plants with Chessington Zoo in return for zebra, lion and elephant manure, considered the highest quality of fertiliser; nowadays, they use horse dung from the farm's own stables.

THE OUTDOOR GYM

The first age of Homo sapiens – which lasted for around 190,000 years, nearly the entire history of the species – was forager and hunter-gatherer; the second, a mere 10,000 years, was about farming and herding. But as of the past two hundred years, we are now firmly ensconced within our third age – the urban labourer and office worker. Consequently, the need to exercise is greater than ever. But there is something Orwellian about the sight of rows and rows of runners, tethered to machines with wires, eyes fixed to yet more screens. For many, it's the feeling of running to get nowhere that fundamentally jars.

However, the recent rise of Green Gyms has found a way to combine exercise with both immersion in the natural world and with the motivation of a tangible outcome. All across the UK, Green Gym enthusiasts from a wide range of backgrounds congregate in random spots, presented with an onerous but important conservation task that will guarantee physical exertion. Typical Green Gym jobs might include cutting back an overgrown pathway or repairing dry stone walls. Willow Farm in Cambridgeshire even offers bowls of soup in exchange for manual potato harvesting. Sessions typically last half a day, preceded by warm-up exercises.

It is also the social aspect that attracts many Green Gym regulars – the opportunity to engage with others, in sharp contrast to the isolated experience of the typical indoor gym. Research has also shown that working at an activity at a pace that suits the individual participant is better for improving cardiovascular fitness and muscular strength than taking part in calorie-fixated aerobics and spin classes. Green Gym participants have also shown marked improvements in the cortisol awakening response which is beneficial for health and well-being, hence the ongoing partnership between the umbrella organisation TCV (The Conservation Volunteers) and mental health charity MIND.

Another innovative alternative to the standard gym experience is **Good Gym**, a not-for-profit organisation founded in 2009 that encourages people to combine exercise with doing something good for people. It works on a basic principle – that running to a different part of the city without taking advantage of being in a new location is a wasted opportunity.

There are three different styles of engagement. Group runs involve a 6- to 8-kilometre run with a small group, with the run broken up by a physical task – distributing wood chips to consolidate the pathways of a cemetery or bagging muck at the local city farm – the emphasis here is on being sociable and active. For the resolutely solo runner, there are missions available where members can charge off on one-person tasks – clearing someone's nettle patch or mowing their lawn. Finally, and most innovatively, runners can be teamed up with isolated adults, who take on the role of 'coach' in the relationship – the end goal of each run is to meet with and chat to 'coach'. Perhaps it isn't surprising that the levels of motivation for exercise sky-rocket when coupled with empathetic behaviour of this variety.

The NHS advises that, on a weekly basis, people do either seventy-five minutes of strenuous exercise, such as running or playing football, or 150 minutes of moderate exercise, such as walking or gardening. Gardening is quite capable of burning the calories in a more sustained and steady fashion. Regular gardeners report not only feeling fitter and having

Boot campers in Finsbury Park

better toned forearms, thighs and bottoms, but more fundamentally, they recognise a positive psychological impact. Gardening has been shown to reduce stress and even help with depression – the experience of interacting with green spaces can be the antidote to the sometimes overwhelming pressures of the way we live in busy cities.

CONSERVATION IN ACTION

According to new research carried out by the Green Exercise Team at the University of Essex, volunteers on wildlife and conservation projects benefit from significant boosts to their mental health. The report tracked people across England taking part in projects ranging from nature walks and conservation work to the Men in Sheds project run by Age UK, which makes bird tables and bug hotels. The tangible evidence that volunteering in wild places can be transformational for participants with low mental well-being has led to proposals that the current burden on the NHS might be alleviated by a new model of caring for people. Despite the value of the UK's green spaces being estimated at around £30 billion a year in terms of health and welfare – on both physical (through the provision of areas for people to exercise) and psychological (their ability to lift people's spirits) grounds – this is being consistently overlooked by the country's decision-makers. The impact of nature on people's health isn't yet beyond a strong association and needs to be conclusively evidenced before GPs can start to act accordingly, but so-called 'social prescribing', the enabling of medical professionals to refer people to local, non-clinical services – for example, conservational organisations – is on the rise.

Perhaps unsurprisingly for such a green city, there is an abundance of volunteering opportunities across London on a daily basis. Some of the major players include **FoodCycle**, who take good food that would otherwise be thrown away and use it to operate community cafés for people with low incomes; **Sustrans**, the UK's leading sustainable transport charity, whose vision is a world in which people choose to travel in ways that benefit their health and the environment; and the **Royal Society for the Protection of Birds** (**RSPB**), who actively look for enthusiasts to share their love of wildlife with the general public.

Like environmental superheroes, **The Conservation Volunteers** (**TCV**) have geographically specific Biodiversity Action Teams (BATs), who offer full-day volunteering experiences on sizeable projects, which can take up to a few weeks in their entirety. With BAT North in King's Cross, BAT South in Lambeth and BAT East in Waltham Forest, the work is varied but might involve a day of hornbeam coppicing in a woodland or building a softwood-sleeper retaining wall in a community garden.

The **London Wildlife Trust** (**LWT**) hosts practical conservation activities for armies of volunteers, as well as suggesting different ways that voluntary conservation activity can be carried out at home or in the garden. Examples of the larger projects include two 'lost London' projects: firstly, the Great North Wood, once a sprawling ancient landscape in south London between Deptford and Selhurst, where the project aims to bring it back to life through enhanced knowledge, improvements to habitats and monitoring of specific woodland species; secondly, the Lost Effra project in Lambeth, where residents are being encouraged to create green landscape features in order to increase local climate resilience – the Effra is a hidden river that continues to wind its way through London's sewers, meaning that where it is very built up and concreted, heavy rainfall can result in flooding. Running through a lot of this work is the aim of reconnecting a population with an ecosystem that is often invisible or at least hidden.

Thames21 is another important ecological outfit that fundamentally believes in the importance of the relationship between a community and its rivers. They task themselves and their thousands of volunteers with the cleaning of London's 400-mile network of waterways and the creation and management of various water-based habitats for wildlife. Project names such as Litter Heroes and The Big Clean-Up speak for themselves.

One of the most significant contributors to modern-day conservation and one that places a huge onus on the individual is citizen science – the collection of data relating to the natural world by the general public, in collaboration with professional scientists. A naturalist is now defined in the *Oxford English Dictionary* as 'an amateur concerned more with observation than with experiment' – it is that power of observation of the simplest data that is enabling the experts to understand the city's wild and to lobby and campaign appropriately on its behalf.

The annual **RSPB Big Garden Birdwatch** is the world's largest wildlife survey. Every year, on a weekend in January, around half a million birdwatchers peer into their gardens for one hour and meticulously scribble down every species that they see. A number of vulnerable species are also monitored through schemes such as these; LWT's **Urban Urchins** aims to reverse the decline of the urban population of hedgehogs; the **Bumblebee Conservation Trust** will empower BeeWatchers; and the PlantTracker app helps volunteers weed out invasive plant species.

A **BioBlitz** is the simplest way to help out on your own green patch – it basically involves an intensive field study over a continuous period of time, counting all the life seen within a defined square. To help sharpen the senses, short courses are run on identifying different species groups, from butterflies to mosses, and there are local wildlife societies on almost everything, ranging from the **Earthworm Society of Britain** to the **Bees, Wasps and Ants Recording Society (BWARS)**.

Nunhead Cemetery summer fair

WET AND WILD

For the average Londoner, the most frequent water-based activity is getting caught in the rain, but London offers many other more pleasurable ways of cooling off in the sun – from total immersion in a lido, river, lake or estuary, to water sports like sailing, canoeing, windsurfing and kayaking. And for those who just want to dip a toe in the water, the tidal Thames presents myriad opportunities for connecting with both nature and history on its shores and banks.

WILD SWIMMING

London's history with outdoor swimming is appropriately one of ebb and flow. Swimming in the Thames itself has been documented for over four hundred years – kings such as Edward II and Charles II were wont to dip in a river so 'clear and pure', as were famous swimmers

Tideswell wild swimming

like Stanley Spencer, Margaret Rutherford and Charles Dickens, who plunged in headfirst at Richmond 'to the astonishment and admiration of all beholders'.

By the 1930s, there were bathing houses, floating baths, beaches and numerous lidos across the capital full of baggy-costumed swimmers. However, in 1957, the Natural History Museum declared the Thames 'biologically dead'. At the time, the *Guardian* reported: 'The tidal reaches of the Thames constitute a badly managed open sewer. No oxygen is to be found in it for several miles above and below London Bridge.' The issue was that the Blitz had destroyed some of the Victorian sewers that previously had helped to keep the river clean, and not everyone felt that the limited post-war resources should be diverted to rectifying the situation.

It wasn't until the 1960s that London's sewage system began improving; a wave of environmental consciousness in the 1970s and 1980s further contributed to the purification of the city's main waterway. These days, the Thames boasts 125 species of fish, a resurrection from a near-total absence in the 1950s, and the river is now busier than it has ever been. There are currently seventeen lidos and outdoor pools in London, and the launch of a successful Kickstarter campaign to create the Thames Baths Lido – a floating pontoon filled with river water but filtered through a bespoke filtration system – seems to indicate a new tide of optimism for outdoor swimming and a reclaiming of the Victorian era of riverside swimming.

Lidos, Ponds and Lakes

Other established London staples include **Charlton Lido** in south-east London, heated to 25°C all year round; the hipster hang-out **London Fields Lido**, on the site of the original 1930s pool; **Tooting Bec Lido**, the largest outdoor pool in Europe – 90 metres of water, meaning even on the busiest day there is room to swim; and the beautiful **Brockwell Lido**, its squat, symmetrical buildings true to the art deco period.

London Fields Lido

For those who prefer to swim on the wilder side, there are the ponds of **Hampstead Heath** – mixed, men's and ladies' – each of the three offering a surreal but reassuring air of escape from the real world. In the summer, the clearings near the men's ponds are strewn with sunbathing men in Speedos – some cook food on barbecues, some read books, some look for nuthatches in the nearby hawthorn, some just people-watch. Once these crowds have been navigated, a large concrete changing area butts up against a closed-off nude area, past which a long jetty and diving board beckons to the ice-cold water.

In particular, the **Kenwood Ladies' Pond** is a private oasis surrounded by trees, honeysuckle and even kingfishers, and has proven a place of security and consistency for many women over the years. Over at Hyde Park, members of the **Serpentine Swimming Club** have been swimming wild in the lake since 1864, come rain or shine, and in 2012 the Serpentine made its debut as an Olympics venue, hosting the triathlon and the men's and women's marathon swim.

River Wey

While the Thames might not seem the obvious destination for sun-kissed beaches, the more intrepid explorers will uncover hidden gems – one of which is near the village of Tilford on the River Wey, one of the many tributaries feeding London's primary waterway. The Wey was one of the first British rivers to be made navigable in the seventeenth century and acted as a power source of twenty-two mills – some of them so old as to have been recorded in the Domesday Book.

For the more adventurous, an 8-mile walk from Chilworth to Guildford takes in an area of wild scrub and gorse, before giving way to more approachable pasture and a village green. The small sandy beach of the **Wey Navigation** appears early on in the walk; there is also another closer to Guildford, with a more extensive sandy beach and a steep sandy bank – rowing boats and canoes are also available to hire from **Farncombe Boat House**. For those coming by train, the River Tillingbourne leads northwards to the Wey Navigation from Shalford railway station.

The shallowness of the water and the gentle slope of the beach make the Wey spot perfect for family swims, and the surrounding area, the Surrey Hills, is one of outstanding beauty. At the river next to the **Barley Mow** pub in Tilford, families paddle in knee-deep clear water under the picturesque stone bridge. Nearby, teenagers jump from the bridge in Shalford Park – the keen swimmer can actually swim all the way from Godalming to Guildford, about 5 miles in total, with one lock to navigate along the way.

Towards Farnham, the **Frensham Great Pond**, another great wild swimming spot, looks like a natural lake but is in fact artificial, dug out in the Middle Ages as a fishpond for the Bishop of Winchester. From the Wey swimming spot, a track goes to Priory Lane and continues to Little Frensham Pond. A track extends uphill towards the A287 before which a waymarked path left leads onto and across the road to the Great Pond. Forest tracks, covered with pine needles, meander from the carpark down towards the water, giving way to clean sandy beaches. The beach, an oasis that feels a long way from the city, is well kept – but the second beach along the bay is more secluded and quieter. Both have official swimming areas, cordoned off, but with a careful look-out for the odd boat, swimmers can venture beyond away from the screams of excited children.

London Royal Docks

For a more urban wild swim, the Royal Docks, near London City Airport and the Excel Centre in east London, feature a former shipping hub converted into open water swimming pools. As ever, the temperatures are bracing – around 18°C (compared to the 25–30°C standard for indoor swimming pools). The pools cater for both the casual swimmer and the serious swimmers in training, with 400-metre, 750-metre and 1,500-metre stretches available. The ponds are part of a major regeneration programme designed to transform the 62-acre area known as Silverstone, previously an area with some of the highest levels of deprivation in the city.

Leigh-on-Sea

One of the more charming wild swimming spots, within striking distance of London, is the old fishing community of Leigh-on-Sea, recently voted the happiest place to live in the UK. Unlike nearby Southend-on-Sea, which is more rollercoasters, casinos and clubs, to enter Old Leigh is to walk back in time – it almost has the feel of a film set medieval town, with its narrow streets, its asymmetrical alleyways winding down to the beach past timber-framed houses and its pubs. It's small, so very discoverable in a couple of hours, and stop-offs must feature artisan gin from the **Crooked Billet** and cockles, mussels and crayfish in a takeaway container from **Osborne Bros**, a family-run business that has been operating in an eighteenth-century stable mews shed since 1880.

Leigh sands are arguably some of the UK's best beaches, less than a mile from the Thames shore. The tide sweeps in and out twice daily, leaving sandy spits and islands deserted for large parts of the day, and the mud flats are a good place to indulge in the healing powers of mud baths. A creek provides access to the sea at all tide levels, a good spot for youngsters and less confident swimmers to sample the water, and four ancient tracks, known as the Cockle Paths, become accessible on the ebb tide for foragers, wild swimmers and bait diggers – the Crowstone Path is best for creek dips, mud baths and oyster foraging.

Over at **Two Tree Island**, marsh samphire (otherwise known as sea asparagus) can be picked between June and August on the foreshore; there are also eel grass shallows on the west tip that fill with water for bathing as the tide rises. Even with the tide out, there are shallow basins on Leigh's beaches that defy the escaping tide, perfect for rolling up the trousers and paddling in shin-high muddy waters.

The surrounding area is full of opportunity for wild pursuits – cycling on **Prittle Brook**, kitesurfing at **Shoebury East Beach** on the uniquely shallow waters of the Thames Estuary and walking the **Saffron Trail**, which in its entirety is a 71-mile footpath from Southend-on-

Sea to Saffron Walden itself, by way of riverside walks, historic monuments and woodlands. The nearby **Hadleigh Country Park** was chosen as London 2012's olympic venue for mountain biking due to its challenging terrain, and the ruins of Hadleigh Castle date back to the thirteenth century.

MUDLARKING

On account of being anaerobic (without oxygen), the Thames preserves whatever it consumes in its variety of muds, making its 95-mile foreshore one of the most sought-after archaeological 'digs' in the UK. On any given day, that foreshore is as covered with so-called mudlarks as it is the artefacts they are sniffing out. Until the twentieth century, mudlarking was a recognised occupation, but these days it is pursued by passionate amateurs. In the past, mudlarkers were traditionally children, some as young as eight. They were typically from the poorest level of society, scrabbling around for possessions accidentally dropped by people getting in and out of boats.

It is important to note the distinction between mudlarkers and beachcombers – the latter content themselves with the shingle, preferring the more solid ground underfoot, so in other words, they operate higher up the beach. Mudlarkers, on the other hand, tend to be equipped with wellingtons and waterproofs, and the more experienced store their harvest in buckets – better protection against a splash of Thames water.

Of the Thames's 215 miles, just under 100 miles is tidal. The section known as the Tideway, which stretches all the way from the sea to the first lock on the river, in Teddington, includes the Thames Estuary, the Thames Gateway and the Pool of London. The general rule of thumb for the mudlarker is to arrive two hours before low tide – many mudlarkers' favourite spots are only revealed at the lowest of tides – where secret recesses and the darker mud hide.

Knowing your mud is key. There are types of weather that will leave the beach caked in the wrong sort of mud – an opaque coating through which no treasures glint. It's all to do with whether the mud is allowed to settle or is churned up by wind or boats as the tide retreats. 'Good muds' include the sort where a rich blackness lurks beneath the surface, the more compacted, gravelly mud, and the mud disguising itself as a dirt-filled sand.

Sticking out from the mud are fragments of ancient history – the foreshore is nature's own cabinet of curiosities – and often found are pieces of clay tobacco pipe. For more than three hundred years, pipes were sold filled and then routinely discarded into the waters once smoked; pipe-makers also worked along the foreshores and ditched their rejects and leftovers. Pipes dating back to the early seventeenth century are commonly found.

The great irony of oysters is that they were once in such abundance as to be the major food source of the poor – their shells can be found in profusion, along with thousands of animal bones belonging to sheep, cows, goats, pigs, poultry, even horses and boars, harking back to the days of Tudor feasting or the nineteenth-century Foreign Cattle Market in Deptford. Potsherds are also worthy finds – Bartmann jug necks and shards of eighteenth-century slipware.

The serious mudlarkers refer to the phenomenon of fragments assembling along the same tidemark as 'find lines'. To 'get your eye in' is to become attuned to tell-tale signs, much like an astronomer becomes acclimatised to the darkness. Regular parallel lines are rarely a feature of the natural, nor are concentric circles – both are invitations to look closer and often turn out to be man-made. Colour difference is also a good clue – as the umber of the Thames contrasts conveniently with pipe clay and terracotta.

Most registered foreshores come under Crown Estate or Port of London ownership, so permits must be secured and discoveries must be registered within fourteen days; under the

Treasure Act 1996, items identified as treasure must be reported and may lead to a shared reward with the landowner.

The Facebook group **London Mudlark**, set up by Lara Maiklem, hosts the largest online mudlarking community, with 'Spot the Find' photos and tips on identification. The best spots for mudlarking in central London include under the Millennium Bridge by Tate Modern on the South Bank and near St Paul's Cathedral on the north bank. The areas by Gabriel's Wharf, Southwark Bridge and Blackfriars Bridge are also good spots.

TideFest

For many of London's residents, the Thames is principally a waterway that divides the city into a feudal allegiance to either north of or south of the river – both parties claim superiority of pubs, schools and green spaces alike. But each summer, the banks of the Thames host a festival, TideFest, aimed at reconnecting London's residents with the extraordinary waterway itself.

On a number of available stretches, including Chiswick Pier, Brentford, Barnes, Deptford, Hackney and Beckton, riverside stalls abound on everything from wildlife to the dangers of flushing the wrong items down the toilet, complete with toilet basins and the invitation to inspect what lurks within. The likes of the London Mudlark group and other archaeologists lead walks on the foreshore and demonstrate their finds in low-fi marquees; children can get involved with river dipping, netting, water testing and games; and a low-tide river walk often sells out fast – the opportunity to see London from a different perspective is tantalising. Paddleboarding specialists run pre-booked sessions at Kew Bridge, but the fun never strays too far from the conservational manifesto – **Paddle & Pick** clean-up sessions also take place. Most of the events are free, although a few are ticketed, so worth booking ahead.

TideFest mudlarking

SAILING AND CANOEING IN LONDON

London is one of the most densely populated cities in the world – so, for all of its green credentials, its roads are multi-laned lessons in confidence or foolhardiness, depending on how you look at it. It's all very well seeking out the oases of parks or nature reserves or even wild swimming spots, tucked away from the commuting masses, but to travel through London while maintaining a connection with nature requires ingenuity.

Once again, this is where the oft overlooked arteries of the capital come into their own – the canals and Thames tributaries connect great swathes of London and can even be used to commute. Many bank employees already commute to Canary Wharf on the high-speed **Thames Clipper**, and this trend is only likely to grow, with eleven new piers planned along the Thames.

CANUTING
One journalist, inspired by the Canal & River Trust's campaign to encourage the public to use Britain's waterways in relaxed 'real time', coined the term and activity 'canuting', or commuting by canoe. His canute took him from Hackney Marshes along the River Lea, joining up with Regent's Canal, full of narrowboats and school trips, towards Angel. Of course, the reality is that the river close up can be less savoury than stretches of the Thames outside London – there's even rumour of a crocodile frequenting the Lea – but it's a way not only to forge an alternate route to work but to start and end the day at a slower pace and with a calmness altogether lacking on other modes of transport.

Alternate travel company **Secret Adventures** offer night-time canoe trips on the Thames, starting in Limehouse and paddling to Rotherhithe, by way of Canary Wharf, Wapping and Tower Bridge (and back again!). To paddle the Thames at night, away from the intense light pollution of the streets, is to find a different rhythm altogether – with only the sound of the river's tidal waters lapping the bank and the dip of paddle against its currents, a sense of its age and history emerges.

Stoke Newington Reservoir

For the fully natural experience (but still within spitting distance of central London), canoeists can turn their paddling forays into an extended outdoor adventure at the **Almost Wild** campsite near Broxbourne, Hertfordshire, on the banks of the River Lea. Previously an overgrown woodland, pockmarked with abandoned caravans and the remnants of years of fly-tipping, a six-month blitz by rangers and volunteers transformed it into a riverside meadow, enough for seventeen pitches, hugged on both sides by the slow-moving river. The camp rangers take the art of going back to basics very seriously – campers can sign up for classes to learn how to cook fish by wrapping them in burdock leaves and placing them on hot embers, and how to use steel and flint to create a spark, with the help of King Alfred's cake – a black fungus found in woodland – to nurture the light.

Taking to the water on boats doesn't have to happen so far afield – one of the more unusual discoveries is hidden behind Stoke Newington's Castle Climbing Centre, an architectural oddity that used to house the Stoke Newington pumping station, with its turrets and towers a result of the Victorian taste for flamboyancy. Behind the castle lies the **West Reservoir Centre**, 30 acres of water overlooked by a stunning 1930s red-brick former filter house. Its double-height rooms are dissected by imposing steel columns and a timber pontoon extends out over the reservoir, zoning the water into open water swimming and water polo areas. A large fleet of dinghies means that all levels of sailing proficiencies are catered for, and with decent winds picking up on certain days, the pond is flocked with white sails tacking past the dog walkers and joggers who make their way up the feeder waterway along its west bank.

The **Brent Reservoir** in north-west London offers a mile-long stretch of water for sailing, including classes available for children, and is part of a 170-hectare area of open water, marshes, trees and grassland designated as a Site of Special Scientific Interest. There is also a small area specifically aimed to encourage children to discover the outdoors, with activities ranging from pond dipping, wildlife observation and mini-beast hunting.

In south-east London, **Shadwell Basin** features an outdoor activity centre in one of London's historic docks; its access to the currents of the Thames makes for more adventurous conditions, while in south-west London, the **Tamesis Club**, located between Kingston Bridge and Teddington Lock, offers a full range of sailing classes, races and social events.

Kayaking in Shadwell Basin

CYCLE RIDES

London is a city that loves to cycle, and if former mayor Boris Johnson has a positive legacy, it lies in his encouraging the city's inhabitants to get on a bike. If they don't own one, they can borrow one of his eponymous Boris bikes (aka **Santander Cycles**) or the dockless **oBikes** (which can be located via a smartphone app and left, well, anywhere).

The celebration of cycling in the capital does not end there – September sees the annual festival of cycling, **RideLondon**, and in the summer there are two big cycle rides, the **London to Brighton** and the overnight **Dunwich Dynamo**, from London to Suffolk. For the more eccentric cyclist, the **Tweed Run** in May is a jaunty metropolitan ride where participants don their sartorial best – tweed and other period clothing – and ride on vintage bicycles (ending with a jolly knees-up), **Critical Mass** is an opportunity to reclaim the streets in a monthly political protest ride, and the **World Naked Bike Ride** in June is held annually across seventy cities in twenty different countries.

Finsbury Park

While cycling London's streets may seem like a death wish to some, there are many cycle paths in London that are not confined to its busy roads, but instead meander through parkland, along vast stretches of canals and past disused railways, joining up the dots of the capital's green spaces. London's cycle paths range from the family-friendly to those suited to the more committed adventurer.

THE WANDLE TRAIL

This well-signed towpath trail noses its way along the entire 9 miles of the River Wandle, a gentle tributary that flows from **Wandle Park** in Croydon (only restored to the surface as recently as 2012) to Wandsworth, where it joins the Thames. A small mill wheel symbol navigates the cyclist or walker through parks and nature reserves, over bridges and tramlines, past city farms and, as you might hope, a smattering of beautiful watermills – in fact, Merton Abbey Mills, between South Wimbledon and Colliers Wood, has one of London's only fully working Grade II listed waterwheels. On the trail's bank, across from the unabating beat of the wheel's great wooden paddles, lies a blue plaque that reads: 'A shy birdwatcher / Photographs 120 species of birds / Likes the 3 species of woodpecker / Occasionally spots a kingfisher.'

Even when it strays from the picturesque, this trail typifies the allure of the urban wild, consistently squeezed between the water on one side and the industrial sprawl on the other – where, in juxtaposition with nature, towers of empty shipping containers or giant concrete bakeries form an intriguing backdrop. Even the water itself surprises at every turn, from the energy of mini waterfalls to the languid beauty of watercress lagoons. But all the way along, its depths attract a profusion of birdlife – groups of coot nibbling at the algae, the stately silhouette of the grey heron and, at the right time and place, the blue flash of a kingfisher at work.

Morden Hall Park

For a more guaranteed slice of the wild, **Deen City Farm**'s barn owl stares resentfully out at the hordes of children who swap, like top trumps, the menagerie of ferrets, rabbits and guinea pigs. In summer, statuesque sunflowers and bushy, pink-tipped sedum nestle among the chicken pens, lending the farm a touch of the countryside.

As well as natural wonders, the trail also does man-made installations – a plethora of unusual bridges and walkways vary the river crossings. The Round Bridge offers two sides of a polo-shaped platform, curved around a grey-ribbed cage, through which you can stare at the rapids below. In another spot, an elevated boardwalk cantilevers out over the water. Both of these structures form part of the **Wandle Art Trail**, created by Andrew Sabin in 2012, with the help of five students from Chelsea College of Art.

But some of the most striking architecture and indeed nature can be found in **Morden Hall Park**, which is arguably the Wandle Trail's crowning glory. Dotted about the park are ivy-covered folly bridges, spanning the river with as many as four arches, some of them in splendid ruin. A former snuff mill now acts as an education centre, next door to a second-hand bookshop. The estate has a fascinating history – the eccentric bachelor owner Gilliat Edward Hatfeild threw garden parties for children around his estate and planted an iconic rose garden, which features over two hundred types of rose to this day. An intimate courtyard and adjoining café offers welcome respite for weary legs and parched lips.

HOLLAND PARK TO CHELSEA PHYSIC GARDEN

One of the advantages of this scenic and easy route is that it starts next to the Ladbroke Grove central docking station for Santander cycles, invalidating the excuse of no suitable equipment before it can even be uttered. Only glimpses of **Rosmead Gardens**, one of the most beautiful of Notting Hill's famous garden squares, can be caught from the residents' gate, unless the excursion happens to coincide with London's **Open Garden Squares Weekend** or **National**

Gardens Scheme, annual initiatives designed to open private gardens of particular renown or interest to the public. The gardens still abide by ancient bye-laws, which include that no person suffering from any infectious disease shall use the grounds (although this garden does allow 'servants' in it) and that no catapults, arrows, saws or sheathed knives will be allowed into the gardens.

The tiny **Kyoto Garden**, nestled within Holland Park, is a good detour for dramatic shades of blossom and a moment of zen before cycling onto another secret gem within another Royal Park. **The Hyde Park Pet Cemetery** started out as a private 'collection' of former pets belonging to the gatekeeper for Victoria Lodge as early as 1881. Mr Winbridge, the original owner of the garden but not of Cherry, its first permanent resident, continued to play host to more and more dogs, and even acted as priest and undertaker to the dozens typically killed under the hooves of carriage horses. The cemetery closed in 1903 but still sports three hundred miniature gravestones, with names ranging from Wobbles to Smut. The cemetery opens to the public by way of private tour, booked through the Royal Parks website.

The final stop is a carefully cultivated and inspiring collection within the **Chelsea Physic Garden**. The garden operates within a microclimate, due to its south-facing aspect, and the shelter provided by tall buildings on three of its sides and the warm air flowing from the river on its fourth. As a consequence, since the seventeenth century (when it was known as the Apothecaries' Garden) it has been used to develop and create new medicines through the understanding of herbs and plants; it now features 5,000 species, including the largest outdoor fruiting olive tree in Britain and an avenue of sweet peas.

Locals come to sit near the oldest man-made rock gardens in Europe (some of the rocks were once part of the Tower of London), seek shade behind the greenhouses (classified according to continent) or to take a lesson in botany from the meticulous classification of every plant. The garden is not only a tribute to the fact that 80 per cent of the world's population now use

herbal medicine as their main source of healthcare, but, with the plants' countries of origin representing every corner of the globe, also a symbol of London's diversity. However while its gardens represent centuries of learning and homeopathic practice, one thing that hasn't changed in three years is the price of the rent – still only £5 a year, quite the best real estate value in all of London, let alone Chelsea. Unfortunately it costs somewhat more to visit!

THE OLYMPIC PARK TO EPPING FOREST

This route travels from one of the most built-up areas of London, the air still strong with the smell of regeneration, to one of the wildest areas, almost entirely untouched by man. Hackney Wick is crammed with character – the canal towpath that follows the River Lea passes row after row of houseboat, and this is an area that has seen an 85 per cent annual increase in residential moorings, in response to the increased challenge of getting onto the London property ladder. This is a mixed community, from start-up entrepreneurs to retired couples, each rooftop aesthetic painting a different story to the passing cyclist.

On the other side of the towpath, the walls of the 1970s warehouses that front the canals have become ripe targets for graffiti in recent years, and this area has fast become the place to see some of London's finest street art. The grotesque clownish grins of Sweet Toof's artwork, as well as the signatures of Himbad and Mighty Mo peer down from the walls, a concrete jungle of colour. It's arguably a bit early in the ride for pit stops, but the riverside benches of the Princess of Wales and The Anchor & Hope pubs spill out invitingly onto the pathway along the way.

The wildness starts to ramp up on next stage of the ride with **Springfield Park** stretching upwards to the left, a children's adventure playground giving way to the Lea Rowing Club, where scullers unzip the water's surface as they pass. The path winds its way up the side of the newly opened **Walthamstow Wetlands**' western most reservoir and on through **Tottenham**

Chelsea Physic Garden

Marshes, until finally it arrives, by way of the traffic-congested Lea Valley Road, in Epping Forest. At 6,000 acres it is the largest public open space in the London area, stretching 12 miles from Manor Park in east London to just north of Epping in Essex. Most of it is designated both a Site of Special Scientific Interest and a Special Area of Conservation, so it provides one of the best opportunities in the capital to be fully immersed in nature.

To really experience what Epping Forest has to offer, mountain bikes are your best bet, especially as the forest is home to the only real mountain biking trails within London. It also contains some of the best single track (track only the width of a bike) in the South East and London – although not always the easiest, as the winter rains transform tracks into thick mud and summer growth throws brambles and low-hanging branches into range. Maps or guides are essential, as the routes aren't signposted. It's not all for the adventurous; there are plenty of gentle hills through leaf-covered trails, with a suitable smattering of tea rooms along the way to quench your thirst.

THE TAMSIN TRAIL

The approach to the Tamsin Trail, which hugs the outer boundary of **Richmond Park**, can be made from every direction along a Thames towpath, starting the immersion into the wilder side as early as possible. Either way, the trail itself, a 7.5-mile loop, is completely devoid of any traffic and guides the cyclist on light-dappled gravel pathways through woodlands and past historic buildings.

Richmond Park

There are multiple entrances – Roehampton Gate, Robin Hood Gate, Kingston Gate, Ham Gate, Richmond Gate and East Sheen Gate – and the anticlockwise route is marginally easier, in terms of how the undulating route rises and falls. **Pembroke Lodge**, near Richmond Gate, is an elegant Georgian mansion, its columned portico groaning with the boughs and purple bloom of wisteria, the only concession to letting the wild have its way in an otherwise formal garden. This grandiose building started its life rather more humbly, back in 1754, as the one-room cottage of the grounds' mole-catcher, employed solely to reduce the potential danger of a hunting guest twisting an ankle on a molehill. Over the intervening years, it has been home to an array of aristocrats, the philosopher Bertrand Russell and the so-called Phantom Squad, a posse of motorcycle riders equipped with radios at front lines during the Second World War.

King Henry's Mound, nearby, offers the chance to see clearly the distant dome and spire of St Paul's Cathedral through an avenue of foliage. It has been protected down the ages – perhaps a reminder that part of the unique pleasure of the urban wild is the counterpoint of natural and man-made wonder. To take in the full gamut of man's tributes to himself, a vista including the four columns of Battersea Power Station, the Gherkin and the Shard, can be sought from the top of Sawyer's Hill in between Richmond and Sheen gates – it is worth the detour.

The piercing screech of parakeets as they flash lime-green overhead accompanies the national collection of azaleas in the **Isabella Plantation**, with peak flower in late April and early May. Finally **Ham House and Garden**, on the west side of the loop, are worth a deviation, via the much-feted restaurant and garden centre **Petersham Nurseries**. The loop is also a decent walk – about two hours at a brisk pace or between three and four hours including stops for photography and sustenance.

PARKLAND WALK – FINSBURY PARK TO ALEXANDRA PALACE

You'd be forgiven for failing to notice the southernmost entrance to London's **Parkland Walk** – a relatively subtle exit on Finsbury Park's west border, nestled between tennis and basketball courts. A high-walled steel bridge looms out of nowhere, crossing the railway tracks below, before lurching right onto the pathway itself, once part of the London and North Eastern Railway's line from Finsbury Park to Edgware. The railway was closed in 1970; in 1984 the tracks were removed along with many of the platforms and station buildings. However, the earlier part of the walk still has the now-overgrown remains of abandoned platforms, remnants of the defunct Crouch End Hill station, standing against the backdrop of graffiti-covered brick walls. Urban myths have it that trains can be heard rumbling along the route close to the Highgate tunnels, even though the track was removed long ago, and that the whole area has been cursed by travellers who were evicted from the pre-Alexandra Palace site.

Parkland Ghosts

In the 1970s and 1980s, one urban legend held that a ghostly 'goat-man' haunted the walk. Children would dare each other to walk the trail in the darkness, and it was perhaps this myth that was the inspiration for Marilyn Collins's man-sized green spriggan sculpture that resides in the alcoves of the wall at the footbridge before the former station. A spriggan is a legendary creature known from Cornish faery lore that can grow from its normal 3 foot-tall gobin dimensions to an 8-foot giant, an intertwining maze of roots and branches. This particular fairy and the fear he evoked was the inspiration for Stephen King's short story 'Crouch End'.

An adventure playground has a smattering of slides and walkways by way of a pitstop for cycling families – a useful antidote to the somewhat eerie feel in certain light. Thick woodland reaches upwards on either side of the trail, only occasionally opening up for views of the surrounding neighbourhood. In addition to a thriving community of foxes and

hedgehogs, sightings of muntjac deer have also been reported. It's not a long track, but this stretch could be in the heart of leafy Suffolk rather than urban London. At the end of the 1.7-mile first stretch, which is imperceptibly uphill, the route climbs out onto Archway Road, momentarily shattering the natural serenity, past the Boogaloo pub. It's worth a quick detour here to find some old tunnels that used to lead through to Highgate station – the tunnels are now blocked up and used as a sanctuary for bats.

The route shimmies through the ancient **Highgate Woods** at Muswell Hill, an oak and hornbeam woodland. The official Parkland Walk continues along the eastern path, but it's well worth going off-piste and taking a look around. Life-long locals can still remember excavation digs in the 1970s where evidence of a Roman settlement was established here. In medieval times, the woods were the hunting estate of the Bishop of London.

It's a climb to **Alexandra Palace** through the park, but it reveals the most panoramic views in all of north London. The park stretches for 196 acres and the palace itself sits atop a hill. Despite opening on Queen Victoria's birthday, 24 May 1873, the palace was never intended for kings or queens but rather as a show of might at the height of the Industrial Revolution. Consequently, it gained a reputation as the People's Palace.

AUTUMN

WILDLIFE WATCHING

As the trees bare their branches and animals emerge to feast on nuts and berries before winter, it is an enchanting time to spot wildlife in London's parks and green spaces. From the fallow deer performing their dramatic annual mating ritual, to mice and squirrels hiding their winter hoards among the fallen leaves, London is teeming with hidden wonders in autumn.

The sheer variety of parklands, rivers and forest, enmeshed within the dense urban sprawl of the city, paradoxically gives London the edge over much of the British countryside in creating unusual conditions for meetings between man and wildlife. One reason for these encounters is London's relative cleanliness – a recent development. In the 1950s, the Thames was declared biologically dead. In other words, the amount of oxygen in the water fell so low that no life could survive and the mud reeked of rotten eggs. But over the last half-century, an intensive focus on habitat creation – from reed beds to mud banks – has transformed the conditions, enabling wildlife to flourish. Feeding otters are testament to the diversity of fish

Opposite: Three grey squirrels in Greenwich Park. Previous page: Autumn sunset, Primrose Hill

and mollusc, rare species such as the water vole have made a comeback at Thamesmead, and even the fragile short-snouted seahorse has been found in the river's saline waters. Sightings of porpoise as well as seal now regularly trend on London's social media channels; on the outskirts of Billingsgate Fish Market, fishmongers have been known to temporarily abandon their stalls in order to foster special relationships with seals who now drift in on the tide. On first sighting of incoming seals, the men clatter corrugated iron fencing to alert them before catapulting missiles of squid and salmon back into the water.

For migratory birds, autumn is a time of change. House martins gather in great numbers around their nesting sites at the Chase Nature Reserve or Fairlop Waters in east London or along telegraph wires the full length of the inner-city Thames. With an epic journey ahead, to their African wintering grounds, they feast little and often to boost their energy supplies. September is the peak month in which summer breeding visitors, such as terns, swallows and warblers, move south. However, as London is a few degrees warmer than the surrounding countryside, some traditional migrants have chosen to remain resident.

London's relationship with its wild isn't always celebratory; rose-ringed parakeets are a species that have certainly divided opinion. Various rumours abound as to the exact nature of their introduction to London – some say that a handful of them were released from the set of the 1951 film *The African Queen* at Shepperton Studios in Surrey, others that they may have been escapee pets in Victorian times that started the now ebullient colony. Either way, the population of parakeets across the country has gone from zero to 30,000 in less than four decades, and when flocks have established strongholds in rural areas, they have been known to strip entire fruit crops. Their distinctive courtship display sees the male sidle along the branch to his mate, repeatedly stretching his wings over the female and gently preening the nape of her neck. Even once mating has taken place, the courtship continues with a delicate linking of the beaks, or 'kissing', repeated a number of times. Not impressed by this ritual or by the liking these birds had apparently taken to his apple trees, James Marchington, who lives on the outskirts of London, created a 'bird table of doom'. He found himself fiercely criticised by the RSPB and PETA when he released a video in which he lured parakeets to a bird feeder before shooting them dead.

Another city-dwelling animal that is met with ambivalence is the urban fox. Anecdotally, the rise in its population is well documented; some claim there are more foxes living in London than there are double-decker buses on the roads. In fact, London's vulpine population, currently measured at 18 per kilometre, is stable and sharply divides its human cohabitants. After a 2013 incident in which a baby's finger was bitten off by a fox in a family home in Bromley (surgeons later reattached the finger), mayor Boris Johnson backed a cull of urban foxes, sparking the commission of legal fox snipers employed at the rate of £75 per animal. An elderly woman, living alone on the fourteenth floor of a concrete council block in east London, took a different approach, such was her desire to reconnect. From a position at her open window, she trained a vixen and her four cubs to sit on command, in anticipation of raw sausages raining down from the skies.

For those wanting more than a chance encounter with a fox on their way home from work, the following wildlife watching opportunities await.

BATS

There are six different species of bat to be found in Greater London; up until recently, experts assumed that the most common of bats – the pipistrelle – was one species, but it has now been discovered that there are two distinct groups that echolocate at different frequencies. One group of pipistrelle bats echolocate at a frequency of 45 kilohertz and another at a significantly higher frequency, 55 kilohertz. In fact the two species, now renamed common pipistrelle and soprano pipistrelle (or '45 pip' and '55 pip'), have been found to show various

other small differences in appearance, behaviour and ecology. There is even a third species of pipistrelle, the Nathusius' pipistrelle – named after a nineteenth-century German zoologist – slightly larger and heavier, whose population swells each year due to migrants from continental Europe. Weighing as little as 3.5 grams, thus rivalling the pygmy shrew for the title of Britain's tiniest mammal, it beggars belief that it flies all the way across the North Sea to get here.

The other bats most commonly seen in London include the noctule – one of the largest bats in Britain and often the first to emerge from their roost, sometime before sunset – and the Daubenton's bat, often called the water bat, as it makes a habit of swooping for caddis flies only centimetres above the surface of water.

Threats to natural habitat are the biggest danger for bats. Despite being protected by law, the constant gentrification of the capital poses ongoing problems. Demolition of old buildings can evict entire colonies, and the fashion for glass façades has resulted in increasingly few settling points for new homes. Light pollution is disorientating, prowling cats are a major hazard and there is even some debate around whether the bats' echolocation is being adversely affected by Wi-Fi signals.

Aside from traipsing around the woods, the best places to see bats are **Sydenham Hill Wood**, **Frays Farm Meadows** in Hillingdon, **Hampstead Heath** and **Wanstead Park**. For the truly gothic experience, the **London Bat Group** organises an annual Moon Phase Survey, where bat counts are held at open areas near water during the full moon.

However, a pickled bat kept in the vaults of London's **Natural History Museum** for thirty years makes London's living population look tame in comparison. The Francis' woolly horseshoe bat, collected in Malaysia in 1983, has spiky, sharp-edged teeth that work like scissors to break open the hard casings of insect bodies.

Bat roost in Sydenham Hill Wood

DEER

One of the great autumnal wonders in the capital is the annual deer rut that lasts from September to November. This takes place all over the UK, but **Richmond Park** is London's Wembley Stadium for the spectacle.

Golden yellows pierce through the shroud of the morning mist at dawn, when the males are most active, making the early morning pilgrimage well worth the bother. An otherworldly sound sets the tone – the combination of a death rattle and a lost lamb bleating for its mother. This bellowing, or 'bolving', from the stags is the male setting out its stall, letting would-be visitors know he's there. The sound is so unusual that it has even attracted human imitators in the annual **Exmoor Bolving Competition**, where men of all ages compete to converse with rutting stags.

Each stag controls a 'harem' of hinds and young, a territory that forms the coveted prize for any rut victor. Along with bellowing, stags also attempt to assert their dominance by lining up next to each other in a 'parallel walk', taking part in the equivalent of a boxing weigh-in. The rut itself is a question of strength – antlers interlocked, the males pushing each other back and forth until one accepts defeat. More often than not, a third 'satellite' male exploits the distraction to mate with some of the harem during the rut. In a bid to look more impressive, stags will often scoop up nests of bracken into their antlers, and the effect is a strange blend of the regal and the comic.

Such is the draw of this ritual that Richmond Park is now as synonymous with wildlife photographers at this time of year as with the wildlife itself. Park managers advise that visitors keep at least 50 metres away from the deer and keep dogs on leads. Other London parks where deer roam freely include **Bushy Park** in south-west London and **Epping Forest** in north-east London.

Deer in Richmond Park

PEREGRINE FALCONS

Arguably the definitive example of urban wildlife is the peregrine falcon, a bird that over recent years has evolved from a rural, cliff-side dweller to a well-known frequenter of London's most famous tall buildings. References to peregrine falcons can be found as far back as Elizabethan times, in works by Shakespeare and others.

> This said, he shakes aloft his Roman blade,
> Which, like a falcon towering in the skies,
> Coucheth the fowl below with his wings' shade,
> Whose crooked beak threats if he mount he dies.

The Rape of Lucrece, William Shakespeare

But the birds experienced significant decline in the centuries that followed, due to persecution and habitat deterioration; by the end of the twentieth century they had disappeared from London altogether. During the Second World War, a directive was issued identifying them as an official security threat, as they would often intercept carrier pigeons and eat them before intelligence messages could be delivered. At one point they were even condemned for being 'in league with Goering's Luftwaffe' and were consequently culled in swathes. But with the feral pigeon's rise in number and fall from grace in the minds of the public (in 2003, they were declared an urban pest), the peregrine has been attracted back to the capital, where its population has soared over the last twenty years. In 2000, there were only three breeding pairs; now there are over thirty, probably the second-highest density of urban peregrines in the world after New York. It's no coincidence that cities with a taste for skyscrapers make perfect

London's falcon population has one man in particular to thank. David Morrison was a steel-fixer on a construction site in Battersea when he noticed that peregrines were nesting in the derelict power station. When the developers needed to take down and rebuild one of the building's famous towers as part of its transformation, Morrison persuaded the company to spend £100,000 on a relocation plan. A mast was built at exactly the same height as the old nest – and the birds promptly took up residence and have bred there ever since.

A peregrine falcon flies past St Paul's

territories – in London, **Battersea Power Station**, **Tate Modern**, the **OXO Tower**, the **Houses of Parliament** and **Charing Cross Hospital** have all featured nesting birds.

One of London's most iconic wild sights is a peregrine hunt or 'stoop'. It takes place at dawn, in advance of the noisy influx of office and construction workers. Watching and waiting from their unrivalled vantage points or even soaring to greater heights, hunting birds will suddenly launch themselves into a dive, reaching world-record speeds of 200 miles per hour. Their quarry, often no mean flyers themselves, can appear to slow down or even stop just before impact, such is the speed that the peregrine bears down on them with.

A WALK IN
THE WOODS

There is something otherworldly about the English woodland at certain times of day – H. E. Bates called it 'the lofty miracle of light and leaf' – trapping the walker in a moment, sometimes transporting them. It is always evocative and beautiful. The towering canopy of trees shields from the rain, refracts the sun, makes endless shadows and shapes and possibilities and, all the time, stands as if reassuringly infinite, with an air of unchanging permanence. There is a palpable sense of life that stretches back to long before us and to far beyond us, and with that slower arc of time comes a rootedness, even for its human visitors. Woods are also a place of constant renewal. At a time when so many wildlife habitats are in decline, deciduous woodlands remain one of the few still relatively rich pockets in the non-human world. They are full of hope and progress.

For a true walk back in time, London's woods are nature's portal. Ancient woodland, defined as land that has been continuously wooded since at least around AD 1600, makes up almost

Hampstead Heath

half of the capital's woods. Some claim that a few areas can even be traced back to the original wild wood that covered Britain around 10,000 years ago, just after the last ice age (it only covers 2 per cent of the UK today).

The type of wildlife that indicates the oldest generation of trees varies depending on the geography of the woodland, although they all share certain criteria for long-term survival: for example, being well adapted to perpetual and deep shade. The tell-tale signs that identify London's arboreal elders include drifts of wood anemone – the plant spreads very slowly, at a rate of only 6 feet every hundred years – and bluebells, which flood the forest floor with a kaleidoscopic blanket of greens, purples and blues during springtime.

Hole-nesting birds are also wild clues to ancient lineage of a woodland – the rattling song and quivering orange-red tails of the redstart, the distinctive bouncing flight of the woodpecker and, harder to see despite their striking black and white plumage, in the very treetops, the pied flycatcher.

But the real connoisseur of ancient woodland is the lemon slug. Unlike common slugs, content to feast in the wake of human endeavour, lemon slugs feed specifically on forest fungi – autumn is the time of year that they are most evident. Nocturnal creatures, they emerge to feed predominantly on the fungal flesh that matches their own colour – ochre brittle gills and butter caps.

Our connection to woodland is deeply ingrained. British surnames reflect the significance in a legacy of woodworkers – Cooper, Cartwright, Wheelwright, Joiner – or description of homes in the wood – Ashley, Attwood, Brayshaw, Foster. Myths and folklore have permeated our national woodlands since the beginning of time; not only Sherwood Forest and its famous green outlaw but also the Glingbobs and Tootflits of Pressmennan Wood in East Lothian, the Gurt Wurm of Shervage Wood in Somerset and the headless woman of Savernake Forest.

It was Sir David Attenborough who captured the importance of ancient woodlands when he said, 'There is little else on Earth that plays host to such a rich community of life within a single living organism.'

London's **Ancient Tree Hunt** trail is a zero-carbon, cycle-friendly trail that takes in the city's spectacular wealth of ancient and special trees. Starting at City Hall in Westminster, it meanders through Chelsea and Fulham to end up in **Kew Gardens**. Reasons to stop along the way include the beauty of the cinnamon-coloured strawberry tree in **Battersea Park**, 'Barney' in Barnes, the biggest London plane tree in the capital, with a girth of more than 8 metres and over a hundred feet tall, and the 500-year-old holm oak in Fulham Palace, as well as sycamores, false acacias, sweet chestnuts and oaks.

The Woodland Trust website has a local woodland finder as well as the ultimate guide to trees, so you can get to grips with the huge diversity of the woodland ecosystem. Another great resource is the Ancient Tree Inventory, a living database of ancient and special trees, which to date has more than 120,000 trees recorded by volunteers.

BLACKBUSH AND TWENTY ACRE SHAW WOODS

Shacked up in the nearby **Downe House**, legendary father of evolution Charles Darwin focused much of his forty years on this home, walking and recording studies of wildlife in Cudham Valley in the borough of Bromley. The valley was formed by run-off from melting ice at the end of the last ice age – the plateaus are clay with flint, the valley itself chalk. On the high sides of the valley are **Blackbush and Twenty Acre Shaw Woods**, which boast a rich variety of plants, including five orchid species.

These ancient woodlands feature numerous veteran trees, notably beech and ash pollards. The uncommon autumn gentian, with its elliptical leaves and purplish bells, can be found between July and September. In the spring the valleys are rich with bluebells, and other ancient woodland indicator species including early dog violet wood anemone, townhall clock, yellow archangel and delicate wood sorrel, whose sleep movements were studied by Darwin. While sleeping is more readily associated with animal life, plants do in fact follow the same circadian rhythms. The leaves of wood sorrel (Oxalis) spread in the day time, while at night time, the leaves fold downward and the flowers close, the determining factor to this behaviour being sunlight. Because photosynthesis can occur only during daylight, the plant conserves energy by reducing its metabolism at night. This topic so intrigued Charles Darwin that he devoted an entire chapter of his book The Power of Movement in Plants (1880) to the subject. Blackbush and Twenty Acre Shaw, and the surrounding valleys, have been proposed as a Unesco Heritage Site – 'Darwin at Downe'.

Darwin developed a method of observation that can be replicated by visitors today who want to immerse themselves in the species that captivated the biologist. His son, Francis, said of him: 'Sometimes in order to observe birds or beasts, he would walk very slowly, just quietly putting down his foot and then waiting before the next step – a habit which he had practised in the tropical forests of Brazil.' Bumblebees were also a particular fascination – his children were roped into helping him map the flight of males, using flour to dust and mark them. His focus was also orchids and butterflies and their cross pollination, in particular the moth-like large skipper, with its orange upperwings and darting flight, and foxes – employing his stealth approach, he had several close encounters and once even reported coming across one sleeping. But the most surprising species observed by Darwin was the black-headed worm; according to Darwin, its role was more important in the history of the world than most would suppose. Each year, a weight of more than ten tonnes of earth passes through the body of a worm and is brought to the surface.

JOYDEN'S WOOD

Joyden's Wood is like a potted history from the Iron Age to the modern day, by way of medieval caves and Second World War memories.

The success of plots like Joyden's Wood relies on the careful planting strategies that are the result of evolving attitudes towards forestry. Following the near-disastrous shortage of timber the UK faced during the First World War, the Forestry Commission was set up in 1919. The primary focus of the huge increase in afforestation was a commercial one – the building of a timber reserve and the rate of return on capital investment was the goal, and growing large quantities of timber in short rotations was the approach. In the 1950s, there was widespread planting of non-native conifers, which created monotonous forests across the country. In the case of Joyden's Wood, it was only once the plot was placed under the management of the Woodland Trust that environmental concerns came to the fore. The conifer trees were felled in favour of native deciduous species such as oak, beech, silver birch and sweet chestnut. These sparser treetops opened up the forest floor to the sky and sun, creating the right environment for bluebells, lily of the valley, honeysuckle and wood sage.

The wood itself is scarred from north to south by Faesten Dic (pronounced 'Festen Ditch'), meaning 'strong dyke'; it is a mile-long Saxon defensive structure built around AD 457 to keep out the marauding Romano-British Londoners. In its heyday, the v-shaped ditch would have been up to 8 metres wide, but nowadays it is only a much gentler, leaf-filled impression of its more impressive past.

Two ponds within the woods are particularly good for newts: the smooth newt, the palmate newt and the rare great crested newt. This was the species at the heart of the EU habitats directive which set former chancellor George Osborne and building developers against conservationists in the build-up to the Brexit referendum. Stanley Johnson (Boris's dad), who was instrumental in setting up the directive said, 'The Spanish have the lynx, the Romanians and Slovenians have wolves, elsewhere in Europe there are bears. I think we should be proud of our great crested newt.'

The wood is full of surprises – including a sculpture of the tail and fuselage of a crashed Hawker Hurricane by a local chainsaw sculptor, to commemorate two Hurricanes shot down over the woods in 1940, and the remains of a medieval dwelling known as the King's Hollow. But the jewel in the crown is the giant acorn seat, from which intones, on the turn of a handle, a poem that seeks to be the voice of the woodland.

SHOOTER'S HILL WOODLAND & OXLEAS WOOD

These two woodlands form part of a wildlife corridor of woodland and grassland stretching from the southern fringe of Orpington, south to the Kent Downs Area of Outstanding Natural Beauty.

Shooter's Hill is an ancient woodland reckoned by ecologists to be one of the most important woodlands for wildlife in the whole of Greater London. It also inspired countless literary giants to remember it in their writings: Byron's Don Juan declaimed, 'Bold Britons; we are now on Shooter's Hill!' when he first arrived in London. It wasn't always a place to muse on nature's beauty; on the contrary, its remoteness made it ideal for highwaymen, hence its name and also that of nearby Gibbet Field. Diarist Samuel Pepys described walking beneath 'the man that hangs upon Shooter's Hill and a filthy sight it was to see how the flesh is shrunk from his bones'.

Oxleas Wood has the greatest population of wild service trees in London – famous for its chequers berries (possibly the origin of 'Chequers Inns'), which can be made edible or, even better, turned alcoholic but need bletting (decomposing) through freezing first. This is a

prime spot for the mouse-like treecreeper, which will suddenly appear, jerking into view, clinging to the base of a thick oak. Probing for food every so often, it methodically works its way up the trunk, moving in a careful spiral, before darting onwards to other feeding opportunities. These woods also feature a decent pond, and are home to the rarest of native amphibians to London, the palmate newt, as well as a couple of large terrapins that can be seen basking on the warmer rocks.

Severndroog Castle, which suddenly looms out of the distance, announces itself as a Gothic medieval tower. However, on closer inspection, it transpires to be an eighteenth-century folly built by Lady James in honour of her late husband, Sir William James, who had attacked and destroyed the island fortress of Suvarnadurg in India, from which the castle takes its name. The view is staggering – on a good day, a total of seven counties can be seen. For the twitcher, it provides a rare opportunity to look down on birds nesting in treetops from above.

For an even closer view of peregrine falcons, as well as newborn lambs, the nearby **Woodlands Farms** is one of the best in London. This is no petting farm though; here, the pigs are slaughtered for pork, the eggs sold, the honey and damsons harvested – this is about the business of farming, rather than education. But it is also the only London farm designated a Higher Level Stewardship by Natural England, which aims to create a mosaic of habitats for specific species and to protect soils and watercourse. Miles of newly planted hedgerow stretch into the distance, offering nesting havens for birds, and a young orchard with pears, plums and apples mostly left for wildlife. The farm only just avoided disaster in 1997, when the Department of Transport wanted to build a motorway through it; luckily a community group defeated the proposal and bought the land on a 999-year lease.

Severndroog Castle, Oxleas Wood

FORAGING FORAYS

The last few years have seen a boom in urban foraging. Barely a day goes by for a blackberry-laden hedgerow without flocks of scavenging humans, clutching Tupperware and plastic bags, seeking to outdo each other. For the forager, there is an inimitable surge of endorphins at the sudden sight of an untouched cluster of berries, hiding within a bush that has otherwise been picked clean. Perhaps it is a reconnection with the tens of thousands of years during which our ancestors hunted and gathered.

Evolutionary psychologists argue that many of our present-day social and psychological behaviours are still in thrall to the ancient forager's brain. That, for example, our capacity to gorge on unhealthy food can be traced back to survival instinct; when our ancestors came across a tree groaning with fruit, they would devour as much as they could, in case it was their only food for a fortnight. While information is scarce about the lives of the ancient foragers,

John Rensten, author of *The Edible City*, picking crab apples in Clissold Park

something we do know is that they existed with relatively few artefacts – a marked contrast to the thousands of objects that govern the modern human's life. Perhaps, then, the act of foraging is on some level an act of liberation – the throwing off of stuff for a few minutes or hours in favour of an unencumbered pursuit in nature.

It would be lazy, however, to assume that our foraging forefathers were in any way less rigorous or intelligent than us. For in addition to scrounging for termites, picking berries, digging for root, stalking rabbits and hunting bison and mammoths, early Homo sapiens also foraged for knowledge. An understanding of their environment had to be faultless, requiring superb mental abilities – there is even evidence that the size of the average human brain was bigger then than now. Collective knowledge is obviously greater now than it's ever been, but on an individual basis, the foragers of old were unrivalled in knowledge and skill.

Thanks to Noma superstar chef, René Redzepi, the procuring of one's own ingredients has reached record highs in recent years. Advocates for modern foraging talk about reconnecting with the land. Living in a world where all of our food comes processed, packaged and cleaned, generations of city-dwellers are growing up entirely divorced from a sense of their natural environment. According to a 2013 survey for the British Nutrition Foundation, one in ten primary school children think that potatoes grow on trees or bushes.

However, a debate also rages around the sustainability of foraging. Certainly, commercial foraging can be damaging, particularly of fungi. Fungi play an important role in feeding wildlife, from deer and rabbits to flies and beetles, as well as being 'nature's recyclers', breaking down organic matter from plants and animals. That said, foraging can also have a positive effect. Some foragers are known to harvest the likes of Himalayan balsam and Japanese knotweed – invasive species that cost the economy millions of pounds every year – for falafels or purée. Growth in sea beet, a cousin of spinach, is also encouraged by the removal of a certain number of leaves.

The moral complexities of foraging have inspired writers from Beatrix Potter to Seamus Heaney. Potter's Peter Rabbit went AWOL on a blackberrying excursion with his sisters and was sent supper-less to bed. Heaney's 'Blackberry-Picking' laments the 'rat-grey fungus, glutting on our cache' when the berries were stored in the byre: 'Each year I hoped they'd keep, knew they would not.'

London is heaving with foraging groups, from **Abundance London**, which meets regularly in Chiswick to the **Incredible Edible Lambeth Harvest**, an offshoot of the **Hackney Harvest**, to **The OrganicLea Vestry House Museum**, a workers' food-growing co-operative in the Lea Valley that has run a scrumping project since 2004. John Rensten will surely inspire foraging virgins with his beautiful book, *The Edible City*, a passionately written daily diary of foraging possibilities in London, and he runs a variety of fantastic courses in the capital and across the country.

BERRIES

Late August, given heavy rain and sun
For a full week, the blackberries would ripen.
At first, just one, a glossy purple clot
Among others, red, green, hard as a knot.
You ate that first one and its flesh was sweet
Like thickened wine: summer's blood was in it
Leaving stains upon the tongue and lust for
Picking.

'Blackberry-Picking', Seamus Heaney

Of the berry family, it is the blackberry that is the embodiment of the foraging season. Late August and September are the ideal time for blackberries but increasingly the familiar black clusters are arriving as early as July and even late June. The best berries to pick are those that have grown in direct sunlight – they should be soft and fully black. Reddish or purple berries and those that don't easily pull away with the softest of tugs aren't ready. Berries along main roads should be avoided, as exhaust fumes can affect the taste, and when picking on verges, it is important to pick above knee height to avoid those that have been urinated on by dogs and other animals. All berries should be soaked in water just before use and also rinsed well before eating or using, but for later use, they can be refrigerated unwashed or even frozen in a container. Blackberries are perfect for making crumble, jam, vodka and smoothies.

> **A few general rules of foraging:**
> - Foragers should always read up on the foraging rules in their local parks and green spaces before setting off.
> - If foraging on a farm or private property, be sure to get permission before you start picking.
> - It's also best to avoid patches that are next to busy roads or have likely been sprayed with pesticides.
> - And, once you've got your harvest, be sure that your fruit is properly identified before you consume it.

The so-called Blackberry Way in **Hackney Marshes** is a single-lane road used only by Lee Valley Park rangers, set against the backdrop of pylons and railway lines. It is an urban forager's dream – that is, as long as a healthy bit of competitiveness is considered part of the fun. For this is foraging en masse. Stretching the full length of the way, this trail attracts every kind of foraging, from the casual 'pick and go' to the family day excursion where semi-feral kids are sent into the less accessible nooks, like chimney sweeps before them.

The best blackberries in **Hampstead Heath** can be found around the ladies' bathing pond, although enthusiastic foragers risk being mistaken for peeping toms. The pathways north of the ponds are good for fruiting blackthorns, or 'sloes'. If looking for sloes, hedgerows are the best start – foragers should beware the sharp spines of the tree. Gardening gloves are preferred

Autumnal Berries in Regent's Park

by some (although trickier for delicate fruit like blackberries), along with good sturdy boots, secateurs or kitchen shears, and long-sleeved shirts. A pair of wild service trees, with their orange-brown chequers fruit, stand as the fifth and ninth trees in a line of boundary oaks, directly south of the Viaduct Road.

Sharing a name with the nearby Category B men's prison, which has hosted the likes of Keith Richards and Pete Doherty, **Wormwood Scrubs** is a 200-acre green space on the border between Hammersmith and Fulham Borough and Kensington Borough. As well as offering foraging opportunities, it has also become an urban birding haven. When the Channel Tunnel took over part of the land, there were inevitable fears about the impact on wildlife; however the trees planted to mask the train lines now guide birds into the park.

Wimbledon Common, with its 460 hectares of birch and heather heath, offers a smorgasbord of outdoor activities, including golf, horse riding, walking, football, children's play, cricket, model boating, outdoor swimming, courting and berry picking. In addition to blackberries, the common boasts a healthy population of hawthorn trees, from which can be gathered haws, bright red berries that are good in a jam. The tree can be identified by its small lobed leaves and long sharp thorns, but haw-foragers will need to arrive early to beat the birds. Luckily the commons are open to the public twenty-four hours a day throughout the year.

The River Wey is in Surrey, but it only takes an hour to get there from central London. The River Wey is a beautiful stretch of river, perfect for canoe trails, with views over the North Downs and plenty of bramble bushes.

Blackberry and Elderberry Jam Recipe
A unique blend of two of London's most popular berries

Ingredients
900g (2lb) blackberries
900g (2lb) elderberries
900g–1.8kg (2–4lb) jam sugar
3–4 tbsp lemon juice

Method
Preparation time: 30min
Cooking time: 20min

1. Wash the berries well and then drain. Strip the elderberries from their branches with a fork.

2. Put both lots of berries into a large saucepan and cook over a low heat until they turn to a soft pulp. Press the berries as they cook to speed up the process and extract as much juice as possible. If the berries are still holding their shape, or are not very juicy, you can give them a quick blast in a blender.

3. Rub the pulp through a sieve using the back of a spoon or the back of a ladle to extract the juice and leave behind the seeds and pips.

4. To each 600ml of juice, add 450g of jam sugar and 1 tbsp of lemon juice.

5. Heat the juice mixture until the sugar has dissolved, then turn up the heat and boil rapidly until setting point is reached. The best way to test setting point is to spoon a small amount onto a cold saucer – if it sets shortly thereafter, it has reached setting point.

6. Ladle into hot, sterilised jars and seal.

ORCHARDS

There was a time when London was so full of orchards that most of the fruit consumed in the capital was grown within them. The modern shopper is probably familiar with, at best, around six varieties of apple. Even then, as creatures of habit, it takes a bout of particular intrepidness to venture away from one's favourite type of taste and crunch. And yet there are in fact over 2,000 different varieties of apple to choose from in the UK – enough to try something new every day for six years.

Orchards have fallen into steep decline since their heyday in late Victorian London, with 98 per cent now gone, but there are still clues to the city's fruit-growing heritage in certain names of apples. Many of the orchards were clustered in south London, a fact reflected in the varieties' names – the Merton Joy and the Howgate Wonder, for example. **The Urban Orchard Project**, originating in Hackney, has launched an important vision of restoring London's orchard scene to its former glory, trying to combat the fact that London now imports over 70 per cent of its apples. Its work has involved both planting new trees and reinstating old sites, using satellite mapping and the help of local knowledge in

Urban Apple Orchard, Camley Street Nature Park

unearthing original ground maps. As well as the obvious choices of apple, pear, cherry and apricot, the project also revives historical fruits such as medlars and quinces. It has even developed a new London apple cultivar and after a public competition, it was named 'Core Blimey'.

Orchards are, at their core, collective spaces and inspire a community spirit in all who interact with them. As with any garden, understanding and contributing to seasons of cyclical growth and harvest is a recipe for well-being, but orchards are particularly straightforward, making them accessible to all. Fruit trees need some initial watering in their early days, but once they've settled, they need little more than some winter maintenance. Perhaps this accounts for the 10,000 Londoners who have been involved with The Urban Orchard Project in its first five years. Harvest, which becomes the centrepiece at October's **London Orchard Festival** each year, speaks most tangibly to both a sense of history and community, with dancing, apple bobbing and storytelling. Late autumn sees the traditional wassail – an ancient custom of exchange originally between medieval lords and their peasants – where orchards are visited and trees sung at with gusto, in a bid to scare away evil spirits and ensure a good flow of sap. The other form of wassailing, door-to-door wassailing, gave way to the Christmas caroling tradition.

In Bromley, the reciprocal relationship between community and orcharding has been taken to an inspirational level. The history of the Bethlem Royal Hospital traces the evolving attitudes toward mental health over the last century. Its first incarnation was the infamous Bethlem asylum at Bishopsgate, but as early as the 1850s, environmental- or eco-therapy became a favourable alternative to more barbaric notions of treatment. When the hospital moved to its current grounds in 1930, the natural world was at the centre of its treatment programmes, with patients involved in farm work and gardening. However, from the 1960s, resistance to the idea of patients working without pay – it being against their human rights – grew, and funding dried up. Finally, at the request of the patients and under its current head of occupational therapy, Bethlem developed a substantial orchard project, paying its patients to mulch, graft and water. In 2007, the charity MIND reported that 90 per cent of people who experienced nature first-hand experienced improved mental and physical health. Now, at any given time the orchard, which is accessible by appointment, sees patients busily immersed in nurturing and harvesting; in the case of the apricot trees, which flower too early for the UK's pollinating insects, patients get out their paintbrushes and pollinate them themselves.

Hampstead's **Fenton House** boasts a 300-year-old orchard, probably one of the oldest in the UK, with a collection of thirty-two heritage varieties. The best time to visit is at its annual House and Garden Apple Weekend in October, with cider and cocktails, and lawn games for children. To the south-east, the **University of Greenwich** in Eltham has recently been voted the most green in the UK, due to its edible garden, forest garden and traditional orchard, all of them run by student volunteers. In the west, the **Mill Hill Park conservation area** in South Acton has won awards for the most attractively presented properties within its borders, as well as for its community orchard, which residents dug through frozen ground to plant in early 2012. And it's not just local residents who have done the digging. In King's Cross, **Alara Wholefoods** have exercised their corporate social responsibility by digging and planting a garden adjacent to a high-speed railway line from St Pancras station. Beehives stand among damson and cherry trees, and from their small vineyard they produce their own wine, Château King's Cross.

MUSHROOMS

Fungi foraging in London has become something of a hot potato. **Epping Forest**, in particular, one of London's prime mushroom habitats, has become a battleground between competitive commercial foragers and, more recently, between the Forest Keepers service and the general public. The rule of thumb across London is a maximum of 1.5kg per person, but in Epping Forest, all foraging is now illegal without a licence.

Historically, the forest has been something of a United Nations, with Italians, Slovaks, Poles and Lithuanians swarming the land as soon as the September full moon draws the autumn's wild mushrooms from the ground. Some of them boast skills acquired as long ago as during the Second World War, and many of them resent the celebrity-chef-fuelled explosion in pedestrian foraging, which has now led to the blanket ban. Even so, it's a dog-eat-dog world among the foraging elite; misinformation thrives, and every trick is employed to get ahead; foragers will regularly say they've drawn a blank in an area where in fact they've found a lot, or worse, they will misreport a haul to encourage rival pickers to head to barren spots.

The reason that fungi picking is particularly frowned upon, relative to other types of foraging, is that by contrast with berries, which have evolved to produce fruit that contain seeds and can therefore be transmitted through the droppings of birds and animals, fungi must transmit their spores in the wind. Plastic bags, the favoured commercial forager's receptacle, prevent those spores from spreading. Fungi are also vital to the wider ecosystem, decomposing wood and plant matter and recycling nutrients, so their removal has a significant impact on their environment.

It's worth noting that not every London forest has taken the drastic measures that Epping Forest has. The safest approach, both legally and environmentally, is to join an expert – Andy Overall, from **Fungi to Be With**, is one of the leading London foragers. Overall's advice is to

One of the most horrifying and intriguing fungus species is Clathrus archeri, aka devil's fingers, which begin their life as large off-white eggs before splitting gently open to reveal a reddish squid-like shape encased in white gelatinous slime or gleba. Four tentacles emerge, as if from a science-fiction nightmare, initially thrusting upwards before then sprawling outwards into a strange star-like formation.

learn the edibles first and then find out what everything else nearby is. Edible species include the pale-blue aniseed toadstool, which tastes and smells like its name; the fragile brittle gill, which comes in three flavours – hot, mild and acrid; or the fabled chicken of the wood, distinguishable by its blazing yellow brackets, which can be made into chips with olive oil. Chicken of the wood should never be picked from yew trees, and even when taken from other trees it should be treated with care. Of the inedible, the most dangerous is the death cap (Overall keeps one in his fridge) – it is common and easily recognised by its dingy green caps, white rings on the stem, white bags at the base and a sickly rancid smell. This species is responsible for 90 per cent of all deaths by fungi, including the Roman Emperor Claudius and Holy Roman Emperor Charles VI.

Another fungal spectacle is most common in garden lawns – for even the laziest forager to observe. Dark rings of grass often appear in fields and on downs, and for many years they invited all manner of speculation as to their cause. The most popular idea, that of dancing fairy folk, was propagated by Chaucer, Pope, Dryden and Tennyson; others blamed fantastical creatures, such as witches and dragons. More feasible explanations were that they were the result of rutting deer or burrowing moles. It wasn't until the eighteenth century that the connection between these rings and the consistent appearance of pale-brown mushrooms was made. The way these fairy-ring mushrooms work is by producing chemicals that inhibit grass growth behind it, but nitrogen to enrich the grass ahead of it, thus creating a ring of lush, darker grass.

Some of London's prime foraging spots include **Hampstead Heath**, **Puttenham Common**, **Wimbledon Common**, **Walthamstow Marshes** and of course **Epping Forest**.

HERBS AND PLANTS

Beyond the popular berries and mushrooms lies a near-infinite menu of edibles for the more intrepid and committed forager. Mugwort, a tall silvery plant, is full of umami, the hallowed fifth taste (after salty, sour, sweet and bitter), often translated from the Japanese as savouriness. Certain chefs are doing their best to champion the citrus-smelling herb, encouraging its use in the preparation of Sunday roasts. You can't buy it fresh from supermarkets, but it thrives along the River Lea in **Walthamstow Marshes**. Yarrow, a pretty herb with small white flowers and feathery fronds, can be used in salads or to thicken soup. Within the spiny stem of the spear thistle lies a succulent green thread perfect for stir fries.

The **Scadbury Acorn Trail** near Bromley, which features one of the oldest oak trees in London, is obviously the perfect spot to find this versatile nut. Acorns can be baked like chestnuts and put into stews and stuffing, made into biscuits and even into ice cream. The flesh of the cobnut can be scraped out and made into a pesto with Wensleydale, wild garlic, nettle, hazelnuts and rapeseed oil. Wild nettles – also the perfect hunting ground for song thrushes – can be used in soup, risotto, spanakopita, and even with gnocchi or fagioli. The challenge is of course to pick without getting stung; the trick is to pinch the stem between thumb and forefinger, start at the top – the most tender parts of the nettles are the top couple pairs of leaves – and work in from the outside.

Granary Square Herb Market

TERRIFIC TREES

In October 1987, winds peaking at more than 120 miles per hour swept through the south east of England, felling more than 15 million trees. From the ashes of that great tragedy rose an initiative to name London's leading landmark trees. Londoners were invited to nominate their local hero. Age and rarity were the defining features.

- In **Ravenscourt Park**, Hammersmith, the **Tree of Heaven**, one of the largest in the country, stands opposite the 'grumpy-looking' tree, a hundred-year-old plane with an overgrown trunk and misshapen branches.

- **The Berkeley Plane**, planted in 1789, is Britain's most expensive tree, valued in 2008 at £750,000 – size, health, history and number of local residents contribute to the value. But every one of **Berkeley Square**'s thirty-one trees is at least over two hundred years old. The reason that plane trees flourish in London is that their bark flakes off, shedding pollutants as it does so.

- In the churchyard for **St Andrew's Church** in Totteridge village stands an ancient yew tree, estimated to be over 2,000 years old, making it the oldest living thing in London.

Tree climbing in Clissold Park

- The **Richmond Royal Oak** is a vast hollow tree – perhaps christened in the grand tradition, following Charles II's ingenuity when attempting to escape from Cromwell's Roundheads. With the Shropshire countryside crawling with soldiers, the king hid inside a great hollow oak tree in the woodlands surrounding Boscobel House, spawning generations of so-called Royal Oaks, and making it the third most common pub name in Britain.

- Finally, the **Marylebone Elm** is distinguished as a double survivor; not just of the Great Storm, but also the ravages of Dutch Elm disease in the 1970s. This tree is the last elm standing in Westminster and still produces flowers every year.

Unlike the Victorians, most modern-day city planners and developers don't fully grasp the significance and impact of large trees in major cities; in fact, many councils are swayed by the perceived threat of trees to building foundations. Between 2002 and 2007, around 2,000 London street trees were cut down following unwarranted subsidence claims. The reality is that for a city like London, so densely populated that on a hot day temperatures can reach nine degrees higher than its rural hinterland, trees are a lifeline – reducing temperature, removing dust and particles, and reducing traffic noise.

The Woodland Trust is endeavouring to plant 64 million trees over the next ten years and is distributing free trees to schools and community groups. The **Tree Council** in London aims to enlist 4,000 urban dwellers to volunteer as planters and tree wardens – a sort of arboreal Neighbourhood Watch. Wardens are encouraged to keep a particular eye on saplings, which are often planted without receiving the necessary aftercare; lack of water is the leading issue, as trees are often surrounded by concrete, and more surprisingly, saplings are often choked by their stake ties as they grow – tell-tale signs are wounded or scarred bark.

CHAMPION CONKERS

For generations of young Brits, autumn has meant one thing and one thing alone. While the tumbling fruit of the majestic horse chestnuts provide the local squirrel population with treasure for their collections, among humans, conkers have always been a tool for fierce battles. Now banned in most schools, conker championships are still run annually in many neighbourhoods around the capital. The annual **Hampstead Heath** championship in north London is the largest (in 2015 it had over four hundred competitors) and has categories for different age groups. Champion conkers can be prepared at home, although methods of preparation have always been the source of much debate and urban myth. Is freezing, baking or even soaking in vinegar the best way to maximise fight readiness? Even more commitment is required to wait patiently for the most promising conkers to fall naturally to the ground; some even reuse last year's champion conker – the older and more wizened, the stronger, so the rumour goes. However, at the **World Conker Championships** in Northamptonshire, all conkers and laces must be supplied by the local conker club, a sort of anti-doping measure to level the playing field.

Sadly, though, the horse chestnut tree has been under threat since 2002 by the infection caused by the leaf miner moth. Shrivelled brown leaves and dried-up seed cases on limp branches confirm the presence of the Macedonian insect. More devastating are the tiny conkers found within, pitiful descendants of their fight-winning parents. Many local authorities are now planting the Indian horse chestnut instead, which is both beautiful and resistant to leaf miner, but produces smaller seeds – so the conker fights that have defined London's autumns for generations of children may one day exist only as fond memory. The fight is not lost yet though – the Conker Tree Science project encourages the public to photograph damaged trees to build up a national picture of the horse chestnut's plight.

THE CAPITAL'S BEST CLIMBING TREES

One of the latest trends claiming to help London's busy inhabitants quite literally rise above it all is urban tree-climbing. With every muscle and sinew called into play and the greatest degree of mental concentration, climbing trees is the ultimate mindful pursuit. It requires the whole body to think. It's also an antidote to the monotony of London's machine-led exercise arenas – row after row of identical grey treadmills and cross-trainers, with the unchanging view of TV screens or, at best, an equally grey London street. Every tree in London is different, with impressive boles, hidden plateaus and knotted limbs stretching upwards, across, even back on themselves.

Jack Cooke, author of *The Tree Climber's Guide* (HarperCollins, 2016), has his five favourite trees:

- The **Kraken** in **Clissold Park,** a horse chestnut where 'twenty friends could happily picnic in the lower branches alone'.

- **Battersea Park's Corkscrew,** the champion plane tree that will reward the most committed with its treetop plateau and looped high branch. According to Cooke, 'When it dies, this tree deserves its own obituary; a chronicle of how the centuries and the saw shaped its curling wings, and a lament for when it is no more'.

- **Highbury Island's Monterey Pine,** which dominates the centre of the busy roundabout island; it was planted on the site of a direct V-1 flying bomb and now feels defiant and resilient enough to deter any such attacks in the future.

- The **Vanguard Beech** of **Lucas Gardens,** which has 'a fairy-tale interior, a wickerwork of branches spun in all directions'.

- **The Granny Pine** of **Paddington Old Cemetery,** which feels appropriately rooted in a sense of ancient history – the tree originates from the Scottish Highlands, where remnants of the forest of Caledon form a 9,000-year link with the past.

Conkers, Primrose Hill

AUTUMN COLOURS

Autumn is a favourite season for many people, and for many reasons. September often brings with it the balmy nights of the increasingly common Indian summer. Later in the season, misty mornings and the reassuring smell of woodsmoke signal the approach of Christmas. But above all, autumn is known for its colourful display – with its explosion of golds, yellows, reds and russets – which usually peaks in London during October. Such is the horticultural superiority of London's parks and arboretums that they are lit up by exotic trees from the Far East, in perfect complement to native woodland favourites such as beech, alder, oak, ash, field maple and cherry.

A staggering 96 per cent of people say that beautiful autumn colours improve their mood – but far fewer understand the science behind the spectacle. It's a question of chemical release. The summer is all about green chlorophyll, the master of photosynthesis – harnessing energy from sunlight and combining with water and carbon dioxide to create sugary sustenance. But once the growing season is out and the tree starts to shut up shop for the winter, the chlorophyll breaks down and is supplanted by other, more colourful substances. It's the likes of carotene, anthocyanin and tannin that paint the classic autumn palette of yellow, red and gold.

Holland Park is the perfect spot to take in autumn colour, with its stunning juxtaposition of formal garden with wild woodland. Most surprising is its Japanese **Kyoto Garden** – known for its colourful blossom, rock waterfalls, koi carp-filled ponds and peacocks. In this garden, donated by Kyoto's Chamber of Commerce in 1991, green leaves are punctuated with exotic pinks and purples; there's climbing equipment, zip wires and giant see-saws for older children, and a fenced-in play area for the younger ones.

To be fully immersed in the spectacle of autumn colour, the **Kew Gardens Treetop Walkway** provides a perspective on the natural world that usually only arborists get to enjoy.

Japanese Aralia, Primrose Hill

The walkway is open all year round, and one of its autumnal showpieces is the northern red oak, whose leaves turn a deep red in autumn. This spectacular tree, also known as the champion oak, doesn't typically fare well in cities, so Kew Gardens affords a rare opportunity to see it flourish in London.

For a more formal affair, **Osterley Park and House** is one of the last surviving country estates in London, once described by Horace Walpole as the 'palace of palaces'. Its gardens have undergone a significant retransformation from modern-day wilderness back to its former glory, and autumn shows it off best – the brilliantly named shagbark hickory does a slightly burnt buttery yellow while the smaller North American Sassafras albidum seems to dip its drooping leaves in a pool of red and orange. Autumnal celebrations culminate in the **Osterley Hallowe'en Pumpkin Festival**, which includes a creepy evening tour of the house.

URBAN
BIRDING

Winter isn't traditionally considered the prime birding season, but those fair-weather fans are missing a trick, as winter offers up a treasure trove of opportunity. With the exception of the bullish robin, birds are typically less territorial in the winter and will flock together in the search for food; bare trees also make spotting easier, and London's green spaces in particular attract crowds of birds that have worked out the connection between humans and food.

By the same logic that many of our summer birds travel south when it gets cold in the UK, thousands of birds come to Britain in the winter to savour the balmier weather relative to their homelands. One of the more exotic visitors – the waxwing – travels all the way from the forests of Siberia and Scandinavia, across the North Sea, to brighten up our least exotic spaces, concrete-grey supermarket car parks. Waxwings are crested with punk mohicans and their eyes are masked with a smudge of black, giving them a vigilante look. They come looking for berries, and when supermarkets began planting berry trees to brighten up their drab exteriors, they attracted a totally unexpected kind of customer.

Barnes Wetland Centre

Male blackbirds come to the UK for the abundance of apples grown here – the females go further south, but the males can't stray that far from home as they'll need to dash back in early spring to stake out their breeding territory. Two species of wild swan – whooper and Bewick's – fly down in noisy flocks from Iceland each year.

More recently, the winter birding scene has entered a new era. Climate change is often a force for bad within the natural world, upsetting long-established cycles and robbing species around the globe of their breeding and feeding grounds. However, in the UK, a recent study has established that milder winter conditions over the last two decades have allowed resident bird species to flourish. A Boxing Day walk is now often accompanied not only by the song of robins, wrens and Cetti's warblers, but also by the two-tone notes of the chiffchaff, the hurdy-gurdy of the goldcrest and the song thrush's symphony. Birds that used to visit for the warmer seasons and return home for winter are now opting to stay.

The Royal Parks are a great starting point for birding – with resident pelicans, tawny owls and kingfishers – but most local parks also provide a much-needed sanctuary for birdlife. Islington's **Laycock Street Park**, for example, supports a house sparrow colony in an attempt to combat the recent severe decline of this once-ubiquitous bird. Open spaces, such as **Hampstead Heath**, **Little Wormwood Scrubs** and **Lea Valley**, are popular birding sites. A growing abundance of birding locations can be found in London's utility sites, typically in former reservoirs or waste sites, some of which have since been converted into nature reserves. Most recently, **Woodberry Wetlands** in Stoke Newington and **Walthamstow Wetlands** have stunning waterways, reed beds and discreet hides. **Rainham Marshes** are home to marsh harriers, lapwings, avocets and ringed plovers. Of course, the Thames and many of its tributaries are great for waders and water birds, and its canals are popular haunts for swans, coots, moorhens and herons.

THE MAGNIFICENT SEVEN CEMETERIES

Some of London's best-known cemeteries are also surprisingly rich in birdlife, providing in their overgrowth a haven to all kinds of wildlife.

Inspired by the Parisian garden cemetery Père Lachaise, London's approach to burying its dead underwent a significant transformation in the first half of the nineteenth century, partly in response to major outbreaks of cholera in the capital. After it became legal to profit from burial ventures, the General Cemetery Company created a loop of private garden-style cemeteries around outer London, starting with **Kensal Green**, then onto **West Norwood**, **Highgate**, **Abney Park**, **Brompton**, **Nunhead** and **Tower Hamlets**; these later became known as the Magnificent Seven.

These cemeteries are refuges for rare breeds of bird and wildlife that might struggle to flourish elsewhere in an urban setting. **Abney Park** is considered one of the most important natural sites in the capital, with more than three hundred species of fungi, some of which are rare throughout the whole of the UK. The great strength of Abney Park is that it has truly been allowed to flourish and mature over a long time and is therefore truly wild, attracting some quite unlikely avian visitors. There are many breeding pairs resident in the park, from sparrowhawks and tawny owls to great spotted woodpeckers and blackcaps. Its oasis-like quality has caught the eye of passing birds of prey, with common buzzards, kestrels, red kites and merlins now often seen overhead, on the lookout for a meal.

Contrary to popular assumption, the success of these cemeteries has nothing to do with the diversity of human remains decomposing beneath the surface, but rather the sheer variety of habitats that co-exist within these protected sites. More than half of the areas taken up by churchyards and cemeteries in London (168 in total) are classified as Sites of Importance for Nature Conservation. The combination of mature trees and open grasslands provide an ideal habitat for birds, but it's the fact that an entire ecosystem can flourish within one cemetery

that makes it unique; slow-growing lichen provide habitats for insects such as marbled beauty moths; ivy, a signature plant of Victorian cemeteries, is an important source of food for over-wintering birds, while caterpillars of the holly blue butterfly feed on its flower buds.

Britain's tiniest bird and one of our native jewels, the firecrest, named for the bright red stripe over its eye, is particularly fond of ivy-covered tree-trunks and features heavily at Tower Hamlets cemetery. It will flit busily from branch to branch, often within metres of human onlookers, sometimes hovering mid-air to prey from the underside of a leaf. It is so small that spotting them can be tricky – the much more common goldcrest is similarly diminutive – but their thin, needling calls help to locate them.

Brompton Park offers regular 'bird walks', including a dawn chorus special starting at 5.30 a.m., but **Highgate Cemetery**, which reportedly used to have peacocks roaming its tunnelled pathways, is really the queen of the Seven, a timeless haven of beauty that marries the life of the natural world with a museum of gravestones, memorialising some of London's most renowned residents. The East Cemetery features the likes of Karl Marx, George Eliot and Alexander Litvinenko, while the West Cemetery, connected by a tunnel beneath Swain's Lane, is a home to wrens, nuthatches, tawny owls, bats and, more recently, urban bees.

RSPB NATURE RESERVES

The UK's RSPB nature reserves are some of the finest, most carefully considered birding sites in the world, and there are a couple of fantastic reserves within the M25, **Rainham Marshes** and **Rye Meads**.

In direct opposition to the voracious appetite of corporate developers to blanket the so-called Thames Gateway with homogenised high rises, the RSPB bought up an 870-acre Ministry of Defence firing range on the Rainham Marshes in the summer of 2000. Originally a medieval

Highgate Cemetery

marshland before it was strewn with shells and hand grenades (now cleared away), this strip of land has that epic quality of flat English coastline, looking out as it does across at the wide expanse of the Thames River at the ominous urban sprawl of Littlebrook Power Station and Dartford beyond it.

There is a stubborn defiance in its untouched wildness, overlooked by pylons and the A13, the gift of hard work by the RSPB, who have also commissioned a unique architectural project to serve as the reserve environment and education centre. The orange, grey and maroon striped container seems to hover above the ground, a guardian angel protecting the two hundred species of bird that flock to the marshes every year. Designed by husband and wife team van Heyningen and Haward Architects, the award-winning structure appears part boat, part barn from a distance, its multi-coloured boards designed to merge into the landscape, like the birds it was built in aid of.

Another example of Rainham Marshes' position at the vanguard of conservational innovation is the fact that it now features the very first RSPB wind turbine. While the RSPB has historically been opposed to badly conceived turbine proposals, it believes that wind power, when understanding its relationship with wildlife, has a valuable role to play in maintaining the capital's wildness.

In terms of its avian displays, Rainham Marshes is now the closest place to London to observe one of the natural world's great wonders, the starling murmuration – thousands of birds perfectly synchronised in a great, swirling, shapeshifting, vortex before an invisible cue signals a mass roost, accompanied by an explosion of sound. These displays were once commonplace in central London – Big Ben was so weighed down by the numbers the bell once stopped moving; even Leicester Square had its own evening show, the oblivious shoppers below taking it for granted. Now the loss of permanent pasture has vastly reduced the urban starling population and pushed the remaining birds further out. At Rainham Marshes,

a flock of between 8,000 and 10,000 birds swirl across the sky at the end of most autumn days. Other notable appearances have included the white-tailed lapwing and sociable plover, the latter hailing from Russia and attracting nearly 2,000 birders to the site.

RSPB Rye Meads, in north London is a smaller reserve, but offers a brilliantly crafted trail, bridging waterways and reed beds with decked boardwalks. Eight hides loom out of the undergrowth to offer birders the opportunity to look for kingfishers nesting among the artificial sand banks.

LONDON WETLAND CENTRE

If it wasn't for the fact that the backdrop to this collection of lakes and wetland habitats include Craven Cottage, Fulham FC's ground, and the BT Tower, it could almost be mistaken for the Norfolk Broads. This site, opened in 2000, is a truly inspiring example of conservational vision by the man described by Sir David Attenborough as the 'patron saint of conservation', Sir Peter Scott (son of Scott of the Antarctic). Scott also established the Slimbridge Wetlands, the Wildfowl & Wetlands Trust (WWT), co-founded the World Wide Fund for Nature (WWF) and, before he died, painted his vision for how Barn Elms, four clay-lined reservoirs that provided London's drinking water since Victorian times, would have skies thronged with wildfowl. What developed from his early ideas was the transformation of one of London's biggest brownfield sites into its newest green open space.

What's difficult to imagine, on visiting today, is how the lagoons and reed beds are all man-made, an illusion made real by shifting 400,000 cubic yards of soil and bedding more than 300,000 aquatic plants and 27,000 trees. Water is piped from the Thames and when it returns, the filtering reed beds it has passed through ensure it is cleaner than when it arrived. The huge shoals of fish that now populate the lakes found their own way there – the creators deliberately avoided stocking any fish so that they could study the way fish colonise such sites unaided.

The three-storey Peacock Tower offers a 360-degree view of the surrounding lakes, a prime spot for its most attractive ducks, the gadwall and shoveler – that gather in such numbers as to be nationally significant – the teal and pochard ducks on the main lake, and the cinnamon heads and close-grained plumage of the wigeon heading for the grazing marsh. Peregrine falcons can be seen diving for a takeaway meal to take back to their urban eyrie on Battersea Power Station.

One of the more elusive residents is also one that all birders long to see – the bittern. Its song, or boom, is one of the eeriest in the bird world and unmistakeable. There are six bitterns on the reserve, which is impressive when you consider that the bittern nearly disappeared more than a century ago and as recently as the 1990s numbers were down to only twenty across the whole country. In some instances, the bittern has been known to flourish by picking off sick or vulnerable starlings and other small birds, tossing them in the air and swallowing them whole. Another elusive bird, the water rail, can be seen skulking among the reeds, its call like that of a squealing pig.

Other hides include the two-storey, glass-fronted observatory in the courtyard – designed like an airport terminal building and providing panoramic views across the entire reserves – the wader scrape hide for wading birds and, in the summer, the sand martin nest bank, which features CCTV cameras that provide a ringside seat as parents feed their chicks. The latest hide, the Headley Discovery hide, has CCTV cameras to provide close-ups on the reed beds, tern rafts and shallow pools.

As if the indigenous population wasn't enough of a draw, the World Wetlands site on the other side of the reserve is divided into fourteen habitats, with birds from around the globe, and examples of the WWT's conservation work around the world.

WALTHAMSTOW WETLANDS

On the other side of London, a sister wetlands opened at the end of 2017, which at 211 hectares makes it the largest urban wetland reserve in Europe; unlike the London Wetlands Centre, however, this one is free to enter.

Surrounded on all sides by the urban sprawl of Tottenham and Walthamstow, this section of the Lea Valley was previously out of bounds, but now waits to be discovered, its huge expanses of metal-grey water surprising visitors with an emphatic calmness. Most of the reservoirs were hand-dug in the nineteenth century; Lockwood, the most recently built, in 1903, took a team of 1,250 men, fifty horses, 20 miles of railway track and all manner of cranes, engines and other engineering machinery. And yet, to the onlooker, these waters feel true to the landscape, as if they are natural lakes that have existed always.

At every turn, the old has been transformed to new purpose. A prominent Victorian chimney stack, originally charged with carrying away fumes from the coal-hungry engine room, has been repurposed with fifty tiny openings for nesting swifts – on its south side, slits function as entry points for Walthamstow's bat population. And ghostly relics allude to its industrial past – an old, wooden wharf loading crane that once offloaded copper ore, brought by sea from Wales; the haunted Ferry Boat Inn, originally the home of the ferryman who transported people across the River Lea. In the old engine room lies the original pumphouse equipment that once powered water cylinders by steam power and then later diesel (it's now a very nice café). And the Grade II listed Coppermill Tower itself is mid Victorian, though there has been a mill on the site since 1086.

But the stars of the show are, as ever, the birds. Walthamstow Wetlands hosts London's largest heronry. As you walk along one of the southern walkways, an eerie line of grey-blue sentinels catches the eye. Erect, motionless, statesmanlike, the rows of grey herons survey the waters for fish, their large platform-like nests silhouetted in the treetops. Cormorants have also been nesting on the site since 1991 – their population peaked in 2004, but if their nests aren't easy to count, their presence is readily advertised by the guano-bleached shores of their eponymous island on Reservoir 5. The same waters are home to overwintering gadwalls, shovelers and pochards, while sandpipers, redshanks and lapwings stop off on their migratory journeys.

THE GREAT INDOORS

Implacable November weather. As much mud in the streets as if the waters had but newly retired from the face of the earth, and it would not be wonderful to meet a Megalosaurus, forty feet long or so, waddling like an elephantine lizard up Holborn Hill.

Bleak House, Charles Dickens

For all the mellow charm of autumn and the hopeful colours of spring, London in winter can be cold and miserable. Grey skies span the horizon and birds huddle against the drizzle, while the energy of plants retreats down into the earth, leaving branches bare. During these months, it's sometimes preferable to experience the urban wild indoors – which is easily done, as the capital's green credentials extend to museums, conservatories, restaurants and indoor gardens, and even upwards to the starry night sky.

The Barbican conservatory

FARM TO TABLE

In the early 1990s, the first wave of 'local, seasonal cooking' that swept the country's culinary scene soon proved to be a fairly short-lived fad. Now though, there is a new generation of 'hyperlocal' chefs who are much more practically engaged with a sustainable farm-to-fork supply chain. The basic principle of the farm-to-table movement is that it eschews expansive supply chains and favours small-scale farming, with a constant eye on balancing ecological imperative with cost-cutting. According to general consensus, as well as earning significant environmental brownie points, the fact that dishes follow the seasons means that the food itself is the very highest quality. And in some cases, the relationship between the chefs and that seasonal produce has been taken to extremes.

The success of London BBQ restaurant **Pitt Cue** has been underpinned by the farming prowess of co-founder Tom Adams. Adams has been busy over the last few years raising mangalitsa pigs outside of the capital in order to capture exactly the right taste and texture of pork so that only the simplest of touches is required once it gets to the kitchen. Pitt Cue started as a food truck on the South Bank and morphed into a tiny but acclaimed restaurant in Soho, before outgrowing that site and becoming an enormous European barbecue restaurant in the City. The key ingredient behind Pitt Cue's metropolitan success is its countryside cousin, Coombeshead Farm in Cornwall, which is a truer reflection of Adams's view on food and farming – a reflective space, far away from London's demanding diners, where there is room for progressive research and development.

At Simon Rogan's farm in the Lake District, which services the much-feted **l'Enclume** in Marylebone (sixteen courses, two Michelin stars), all chefs will spend at least a month on the farm before they set foot in the kitchen – it's all about understanding the connection between the moment something is planted all the way to the plate. The Rogan way is that the farm 'is designed by chefs, for chefs, run for chefs' – not a business first and foremost, so much as a rigorous hunt for the ultimate end product. These days, Rogan's London empire includes **Roganic**, originally a pop-up in Marylebone, now making a permanent return, and **Aulis**, a development kitchen and eight-seat chef's table in Soho.

Other titans of the movement include the Gladwin brothers – Richard, Oliver and Gregory – who, to date, have opened **Rabbit** in Chelsea, **Nutbourne** in Battersea, and **The Shed** in Notting Hill. Brought up on a West Sussex smallholding, the brothers cover all bases: Gregory farms livestock in West Sussex, Oliver is the executive chef and Richard is the business brains. For them, it's not just about harvesting their own crops, but also about following wild food as signals for the new seasons. Wild garlic signals the start of spring; when wild garlic broth appears on the blackboard, the springtime menu kicks into gear. In addition to foraging and using their own farm, the brothers have also created a network of local farms from which they source – a community of like-minded suppliers.

MUSEUMS OF THE NATURAL WORLD

At the top of Lordship Lane in Forest Hill, another former private collection turned public is housed within the **Horniman Museum**; it contains a completely unique array of anthropological curiosities and a particularly remarkable taxidermy collection, set in 16 acres of landscaped gardens. The *New York Times* recently rated it one of the top ten coolest museums in the world, the only London entry in the list alongside the likes of MoMA in New York.

Standing sentry at the roadside entrance to the museum, an eagle perches on the head of a girl who stands astride a bear – the characters make up a wooden totem that was contributed by a Tlingit native Alaskan, based on the legend of a girl whose punishment for cursing a bear family was to be deceived into marrying one and having children – half human, half bear cub – with it. Inside, the walls are lined with all manner of stuffed beasts, from the rare Sunda pangolin to the extinct dodo (one of the few specimens that is not real, as you might expect) and passenger pigeon. At the time of America's discovery by the Founding Fathers,

there were around 4 billion passenger pigeons in the States; by the time the Horniman's specimen, Martha died in Cincinnati Zoo in 1914, the species had been relentlessly hunted to extinction and she was thought to be the last. On the balcony, one of the exhibits is known as the 'flashing bat', its open wings reminiscent of an old man's raincoat. In the basement aquarium, the neon glow of the coral sustains the algae living within the reef by providing extra light and aiding the plants' photosynthesis.

Beyond its permanent residents, the museum curates a diverse array of animal and anthropological exhibition programmes, ranging from the sublime to the ridiculous. In 2006, the museum launched a worldwide search for a huge stuffed polar bear that had been a documented favourite among the Victorian public, but which has not been seen since it was lent to Selfridges department store for a flamboyant Christmas window display sixty years ago. Another display, the Great White Bear exhibition, was the result of an effort to photograph every taxidermised polar bear in the UK and showed bears stuffed in various different styles – including some particularly contorted and misshapen efforts before the 'realist' style of the mid nineteenth century kicked in.

But the undisputed emperor of the museum is the enormous Horniman walrus who presides uncomfortably over the glass-fronted exhibits surrounding him. Now the museum's best-loved exhibit, the Horniman walrus was brought to London by the Victorian hunter James Henry Hubbard, who collected it from Hudson Bay in Canada. When he handed it over to a taxidermist back in London, the stuffer in question – having, like most people of his day, never seen a live walrus – had no idea that walruses feature deep folds in their thick skin. Consequently, he did the logical thing and stuffed it to the brim, resulting in the gigantic, overweight creature that Horniman bought and which is now displayed as the museum's centerpiece. The lines where the folds should have been are still visible 140 years later. The walrus even has his own (unofficial) Twitter feed: @HornimanWalrus.

Stuffed owls at the Horniman Museum

In among the flora and fauna, the newest collection, the World Gallery, celebrates what it means to be human and is full of objects from around the globe. Every Saturday of the year, the museum's gardens fill up with stalls, replete with everything from cherry berry juices to artisan pies and handmade salamis. Christmas sees a selection of seasonal exhibitions including the British Wildlife Photography Awards, sticky porridge and edible snowballs, as well as Christmas markets and fairs.

Perhaps it's inevitable when museum exhibitions are inspired by the wild, but there is a pleasing randomness to the collection in the **Garden Museum** of St-Mary-at-Lambeth church, and a sense that as much significance is attributed to the small and quotidian as to the larger works of art. Like the Horniman, this is a space dedicated to curiosities, animated by the idiosyncratic contributions of gardeners and horticulturalists from all over; from mundane objects elevated by association, like Gertrude Jekyll's desk, to the intrinsically unique glass cucumber straightener invented by George Stephenson. This fusing of the pedestrian with the poetic feels right, given that John Tradescant and his son, John the Younger, the founders of this style of curation and both of them gardeners and travellers, are buried in the churchyard of the museum itself, in a tomb engraved with crocodiles and skulls.

It was in fact two Tradescant fans and garden lovers who, on discovering the church was to be demolished, campaigned for its conversion into a museum back in the 1970s. Forty years on, the museum underwent a major facelift, reopening in May 2017. A two-storey structure houses temporary and permanent displays, with a pale timber that neither physically touches nor aesthetically undermines the original stone of the church walls. Alun Jones, its architect, describes it as 'robust enough to stand up to the church without having an argument with it.' Outside, the touch is similarly light, with bronze cladding designed to echo the flaking trunks of the plane trees (the now iconic London species was in fact introduced to Britain by the Tradescants). The museum's director particularly enjoys its location in a non-gardened area of London, where lots of people live in flats, describing it as a 'clinging-on space in the city.'

STARGAZING OBSERVATORIES

For ordinary people living in the late Victorian era with an interest in natural sciences, public lectures were really their only available education. When the **Hampstead Observatory** behind Whitestone Pond, London's highest point, was established in 1898, London was still lit by gas lamps and 'light pollution' didn't exist; consequently, views of the Milky Way would have been unrivalled. Over the years, the telescope has been kept functioning through the passion and commitment of a few key enthusiasts. It has viewed Halley's comet twice, with thousands queuing up in 1985, Hale-Bopp comet in 1997 and the transit of Venus in June 2004.

The observatory itself is an unobtrusive hut tucked away behind railings – two low-tech flaps are manually winched outwards to reveal the night sky. Inside, an old notebook is full of pencil drawings of historical observations but the main draw is the telescope itself, with its original 6-inch refractor, made in 1898. The whole set-up has the air of a space frozen in time – the Victorian stargazers who once sat against the same palette of wood and metal seem to linger in the air. The renovations that took place in the 1970s introduced equatorial mounting, which means that to this day, the telescope is placed on an axis, driven by a motor that tracks the stars as they move.

Judging by its website, the **Observatory of University College London** doesn't seem too keen on public visitors. Its online rhetoric emphasises that it is not a tourist attraction, it is not wheelchair-friendly and it has no on-site visitor parking; that neither the Moon nor the brighter planets are well placed for viewing, and that sessions may be cancelled at short notice.

However, behind the stern façade, important work is taking place. In 2014, the astronomers working there announced the discovery of a supernova, so-called 2014J, the closest star explosion to Earth in twenty-seven years. Normally, such discoveries are the territory of major observatories in remote landscapes away from urban light – but whereas those rely on software, this cosmic appearance was spotted by the human eye. This supernova is a variety known as type Ia; all type Ias are thought to have the same brightness and therefore can be used to measure cosmic distances and better understand dark energy, that mysterious force. The observatory offers intensive courses about the mysteries and secrets of our 'Ghost Universe' of dark matter and energy.

Winter months are the best time to stargaze from your own back garden, given the sky is at its darkest. The key is finding a dark spot – away from street lamps, headlights, neighbours' windows – and allowing your eyes to acclimatise to the darkness. It can take twenty minutes of standing and looking into the night to get fully dark-adapted. If a torch is needed, its light should be covered with a red filter, as normal light will immediately undo all the good work. And specialist equipment isn't even necessary – a basic set of binoculars or telescope can do the trick.

GREENHOUSES AND INDOOR GARDENS

One of the starkest contrasts between man and nature's idea of beauty can be found at the Barbican in central London. Brutalism, described by Queen Elizabeth II as 'one of the modern wonders of the world' is illustrated at its most extreme and epic by the Barbican estate – a trio of high-rise towers and a utopian vision for high-density residential neighbourhoods. At its centre lies the Barbican theatre, where visitors can experience the work of the most innovative and inventive theatre companies from around the world. The star turn, however,

Astronomy groups flourish all over the capital, and are always a good way to glean local knowledge. Local groups will also have simple sodium light filters to counteract the classic orange sodium light of street lamps. A good test of eyesight since ancient times are the Pleiades, a star cluster also known as the Seven Sisters. In London, most people can pick out around six stars from the cluster; given time for the eyes to adjust, that number can go up to thirteen or fourteen; through a telescope, hundreds can be seen.

is neither the buildings nor the actors, but the 2,000 species of plants inside the **Barbican Conservatory**. This pocket of jungle green, layered and self-enveloping, seems almost clandestine, hidden away within this stone kingdom. Visitors are instantly transported into a humid, tropical world; paving stones lead past overhanging palm leaves to ponds and waterfalls, an impressive transformation given it all started with a few pot plants to hide the building's imposing fly tower. A raised walkway leads to a wooden barrier with views of the gardens; beyond, an arid house enjoys drier climes, having been starved of water between September and March – perfect for the cacti and succulents that twist wickedly against the glass roof, as if scrabbling for an exit.

These are plants that feel all the more alien to the metropolitan Londoner for their textures and size. The giant kentia palm, more familiar as a houseplant, has been left to grow all the way to the roof. Towering above are 16-foot tree ferns, while the notched leaves of the Epiphyllum crenatum dangles from hanging baskets to brush your head as you walk past – in the wild, this orchid cactus would normally root itself in a pocket of leaf mould in the hollow of a tree.

When the site opened in 1982, the Barbican's garden architects attempted to impose a series of raised beds onto the original 1950s design, where the 'heroic simplicity' allowed only for a formal grid of four square planters. Hawthorns grew successfully, along with other shrubs, but leaking soon became an issue. A new design by Nigel Dunnett has supplanted it – a lightweight growing substrate designed to cope with perennial planting. Now, almost 40,000 plants and bulbs and a range of long-flowering perennials and grasses have been planted, mixing natives and non-natives to encourage the greatest number and diversity of pollinators – for example goldfinches and seed-eating birds in winter.

In the ponds lurk terrapins that once caused mayhem at Hampstead Ponds, where they were dumped in their droves once the early 1990s craze for importing them, sparked by the Teenage Mutant Ninja Turtles, had died away. Once installed on the Heath, they grew in numbers and began to terrorise the local population – there were reports of fish, newts, toads and ducklings being eaten, and they even occasionally took on adult grebes and coots. The so-called 'terrorpins' were eventually collected by park rangers – some were sent on permanent holiday to Tuscany, others were installed at the Barbican.

For an indoor garden experience that is more about people, music and cocktails than secluded benches and secret ponds, the **Sky Garden** occupies the entire top three storeys of London's 'Walkie-Talkie' tower, 20 Fenchurch Street. The most impressive features of the space are the vast domed windows and vaulted roof overlooking the City of London. The garden design is supposed to look 'as if you're coming across a mountain slope'; it includes three terraces – based on the idea of the 'evolution of plants' – at the top, a shady forest of fig trees and ferns overlooks a middle tier of ancient cycads, while the bottom level is filled with sun-loving plant species including African lilies and red-hot pokers.

Hall Place and Gardens at Bexley combine the formal – rolling parkland and heraldic topiary (including the giant Queen's Beast sculptures) – with the exotic – crops like coffee, avocado and bananas, in their indoor conservatories, rivalling those at the more famous Kew Gardens.

The designers of the **US embassy**, a 518,000-square-foot building in Nine Elms, have approached the English tradition of urban gardens in a different way. Outside, sculpted meadow terrains wind into the lobby and inside, the six different interiors are each inspired by a region of the States; Canyonlands, the Gulf Coast, the Midwest, the Potomac River Valley, the Pacific Coast and the Mid-Atlantic. As part of the surrounding **Embassy Gardens**, a new district catalysed by the new building, the **Linear Park**, which when completed will be open to the public, is inspired by New York's High Line, the section of former railroad reclaimed as an aerial greenway.

FESTIVE SPIRIT

TREES, WREATHS AND MISTLETOE

At a time when much else is dormant and branches are bare, mistletoe's oval green leaves and waxy white berries offer some colourful respite. It is because it is one of winter's rare blossomers that the Druids came to view it as a sacred symbol of vivacity and it became known for its healing properties, particularly for restoring fertility. The connection between those ancient beliefs and the modern custom of kissing is unclear, although Norse mythology has Frigg, their goddess of love and fertility, declaring all who stand beneath mistletoe safe from harm and instead worthy of a token of love. In some parts of England, mistletoe is burned on Twelfth Night, lest all the boys and girls who have kissed under it never marry. Recently, a group that called themselves 'mistletoeonthetube.co.uk' hung sprigs above the heads of harried commuters, bringing the wild into the most urban of environments.

Clissold Park

Wild mistletoe is surprisingly scarce in London – it works effectively as a parasite and tends to grow on host trees, such as apples, hawthorns, maples and willows. It grows slowly and the plant is often eaten by birds when it is still very small. If it makes it past the early stages, first flowers and berries may not appear until the fourth or fifth year of germination. One of the threats to its growth is so-called mistletoe 'rustling', on the increase due to its seasonal value. In Richmond, the Biodiversity Partnership has an action plan for mistletoe, which encourages propagating mistletoe on suitable host trees in parks and open spaces. It is possible, albeit difficult, to grow your own mistletoe – cut a little nick in the bark of a host so that the flap of bark is facing upwards, then squeeze a fresh, ripe berry with its seed into the space; the rest is a waiting game.

Christmas is a symbolic festival and much of its symbolism is caught up in the idea of life continuing even in the depths of winter. The classic wreath, derived from the Old English word writhen, meaning 'to writhe' or 'to twist', uses evergreen foliage to represent growth and the everlasting. The interweaving of berries, fruits and nuts in so-called harvest wreaths, popular in Eastern European countries, is designed to ward off crop failure in the year to come.

The mistletoe and wreath-making businesses are now epic ones. In certain areas of London, calling a florist to hang a wreath and install a fir tree will cost a minimum of £1,500. The likes of Pulbrook & Gould charge £2,450 for a bespoke wreath, but there is a much more DIY side of the market. Nurseries and florists all over London compete to out-craft each other with wreath-making classes. **Petersham Nurseries**, one of London's botanical jewels, offers classes using the distinctive pale green leaves of the eucalyptus branch, stems of pussy willow and large pine cones. **Columbia Creative**, inspired by the world-famous Columbia Road Flower Market, workshops all styles from rustic to luxury, while the **Covent Garden Academy of Flowers** also hosts table arrangement workshops, riffing on the different ways dried clementines, cinnamon sticks and pine cones can be laid out.

Each year, 6–8 million Christmas trees are bought in the UK. These days, the non-drop Nordmann fir has replaced the Norway spruce as the most popular tree of good cheer – it takes eight to ten years to grow to 6 feet before a brief decorative turn in a festive living room. Even so, real trees are a greener choice than artificial ones, which would need to be kept for a decade before its footprint is lower in carbon, due to the oil the plastic is made with. Real trees also provide a habitat for wildlife to live in as they grow, so the industry itself is enabling, not denuding, a natural environment.

It's possible to buy a real tree in London with extra eco-credentials. Even IKEA has run a deal where you pay £25 but get £20 back if you return the tree in the New Year, as part of its eco-drive. **King's Christmas Trees** in south-east London contributes directly to the care of rough sleepers and vulnerable people through the work of the Jericho Road Project. Many, including **One Fine Tree** in Fulham, **St John's Church** in Kensal Green and **St Paul's Church** in Stoke Newington, commit to planting a new tree for every tree bought. **South London Christmas Trees** in Kent offer the chance to choose your own tree from the planation itself, also offering real honey made from wild flowers and trees on the farm.

A recent scientific survey tested the four treatments that have been suggested to prolong the health of cut trees. Feeding the tree energy drink and beer wasn't successful. Water – cold or boiled – was decent. But the best treatment was spraying the foliage with hairspray – the spray reduces water loss by blocking the stomata in the needles. Of course, the downside is a particularly flammable tree, which is worth remembering.

ENCHANTED FORESTS

Kew Gardens in the winter is a bustling, somewhat frenetic, marketplace for all things Christmas – mulled wine and roasted chestnut stalls line the street that connects the underground with its famous gardens. But the advance-ticket buyer can navigate their way through the excited throng into an oasis of arboreal beauty and calm, with specific entry times ensuring a civilised number of fellow tree-lovers.

The 1-mile nature trail picks up from an entrance through two giant ribbon-festooned Christmas trees and snakes past a series of impressive botanical light installations. A choir of trees light up and flicker in rhythm across from a vast field of domed light boxes on stilts that glow a rainbow of colours at entranced onlookers. Nature is both the backdrop and the theme of this exhibition – oversized sculptures of illuminated robins perch like avian wicker men above rings of flaming torches. Moments later, participants become human bees as they descend beneath The Hive, a gigantic aluminium beehive studded with a thousand tiny LED lights that almost seem to flit overhead. Flickering light and an immersive soundtrack respond in real time to the activity of Kew's living bees. A tunnel of light pulsates neon tracers on every side, transporting guests into a sci-fi environment. The grand finale is a laser beam show over the lake which projects columns of spray to capture the lights above the curved glazed roof of the famous Sir Joseph Banks Building, which houses the 83,000 artefacts that make up Kew's Economic Botany Collection subterraneously.

On the other side of London, London Zoo's safari-style sister zoo, **Whipsnade**, has started hosting a Wild Lights night, where guests can wind their way along a 1-kilometre trail, entertained by carol singers, fire jugglers and costumed performers. The giant animal lanterns that light up clearings along the trail are the only animals actually on show at this time of night – the Zoological Society of London was forced to have a rethink after it cancelled its late-night Zoo Late parties, following incidents involving rowdy visitors which saw one man pouring beer over a tiger. At Wild Lights, the event is very much aimed at family groups, and it's all minced pies and spiced apple juice – much more wholesome.

The Hive, Kew Gardens

CHRISTMAS DAY SWIMMING

Bathing in the **Hampstead Heath** ponds is wild swimming with no frills – a moment where the city genuinely recedes; where beneath paddling feet, plants and reeds drift up from the pond floor and low-hanging branches dangle their leaves and vines into the water.

Every Christmas Day, a mixture of hardy pond-swimming regulars and those looking for a quick hangover cure congregate at the Men's Pond for the annual men's and women's Christmas races – a 40-yard splash in 4°C water. The president of the Highgate Lifebuoys swimming club serenades the competitors with a bugled rendition of 'Hark the Herald Angels' to start the races. This race has taken place on the Heath every year since 1895, come rain, shine or ice, but while a similar, even more ancient swim in the Serpentine has occasionally been called off due to its waters being frozen rock solid, the Heath swim has always gone ahead. Swimmers are encouraged to arrive by 10.45 a.m. – the ladies' race takes place at 11 a.m., followed by the men's, then all-comers and finally, the club race.

Down in Hyde Park, the Peter Pan Cup has been so-named since 1904, when author and playwright J. M. Barrie presented the first Peter Pan Cup to the winner. A man by the name of A. C. Fear, a respected member of the club, won the title, after a bitter struggle. Friends of a Mr Classey were disappointed that he opted not to swim, but given that he was eighty-four years old, they understood his desire to retire. Nowadays, swimmers have to be members of the Serpentine Swimming Club – organisers point out that being accustomed to the icy waters is a survival must, and not to be taken lightly.

BOXING DAY WALKS

Christmas is, on the surface, a moment of the year marketed as fun, festive and full of good cheer. But in reality, the intensity of all that family and food can get too much and an escape into the wild, with all of its restorative simplicity, beckons. Be it alone or en famille, the Boxing Day walk can clear the head and cleanse the body.

Two-Peak Challenge

Getting up high is good for the soul and for reflecting on life, the future and the year ahead. One great north London Boxing Day walk takes in two panoramic views of London, with only 1.8 miles between its two peaks. **Parliament Hill**, on Hampstead Heath, can be approached on all sides and the steep climb makes the arrival all the more rewarding. Dog walkers, joggers and kite-flyers congregate, often hushed into complete silence by the breathtaking view of the city. A few benches haphazardly adorn the southern slope, with couples snuggling up to each other, ensconced in their own private view; it can feel almost like you are observing a photograph of a moment, rather than being part of that moment yourself. To reach the second peak of **Primrose Hill** is a straightforward walk through the food and drink havens of Belsize Park and Chalk Farm, for an even steeper climb to another lofty view.

Waterway Walks

London's waterways are its invisible arteries, and walking the rivers and canals is a wonderful way to see another, often quieter, side of the city. The 3.5-mile walk down the River Lea, past **Hackney Marshes** and towards the **Queen Elizabeth Olympic Park** is a trip down London's most recent major redevelopment. It now uses clever crossings, underpasses, ramps and steps to link what will be six small riverine parks. The unique environment of this walk lies in the fact that, until recently, this was always a back land, a place where the not-to-be-seen was carried out: car-breaking, gin distilling, abattoirs, waterworks – it was a working

area, not a public space. It has slowly been reclaimed, however, allowing the public more access to its water and its wildlife with each step.

Another canal walkway that quietly carves its way through areas of London that, at street-level, throb with noise and people is the 2.4 miles from **Warwick Avenue**, through the Regent's Park Outer Circle, to **Camden Lock**. For some of it, the rear gardens of grand London properties back on to the water itself, some with small jetties and rowboats. The distinctive tetrahedron of the Snowdon Aviary suddenly looms into view over the canal, with the distinctive white ibis lazily flapping its wings to traverse its vast playground.

In west London, a 2-mile towpath heads from Putney Bridge to Hammersmith Bridge, taking in a part of the river that has relatively little traffic and stopping by the **London Wetlands Centre** en route. There are plenty of excellent riverside pubs, providing a well-earned pit stop after a brisk stretch of walking, including **The Dove** and **The Old Ship**.

Blackheath and Greenwich Park

In south-east London, Lewisham via Blackheath to Greenwich Park is particularly beautiful in the winter. A former hunting ground for Henry VIII, the park is full of history, and home to the **Royal Observatory** and the **Royal Maritime Museum.**

SLEDGING SLOPES

Snow that settles in London may be rare, and fairly short-lived, but Londoners go wild for a snow flurry. On a snowy day, the capital's steepest slopes are jam-packed with sledges, toboggans and even the occasional skier.

Greenwich Park

Alexandra Palace is the perfect sledging spot, with gentle slopes for the young ones and more challenging ones for teens and adults. An added bonus is the amazing view from the top of famous landmarks such as St Paul's Cathedral, the London Stadium in the Olympic Park, and much more. Afterwards, fill up with hot chocolate or chips at **The Phoenix** pub in the palace complex at the top of the hill.

The top of **Parliament Hill** on Hampstead Heath is a staple for snow-loving north Londoners, with a sweeping view of the capital to boot. The main drag can get mighty busy (and icy) though.

In south London, try the hill that runs right in front of the Royal Observatory in **Greenwich Park**, and in west London take a turn on the rather grand-sounding King Henry's Mound in Richmond Park, after which you can thaw out with a hot chocolate at **Pembroke Lodge**.

Clissold Park

DIRECTORY
& USEFUL ADDRESSES

BUTTERFLY HOUSES

Horniman Museum and Gardens
100 London Road, Forest Hill, SE23 3PQ
020 8699 1872
www.horniman.ac.uk

Natural History Museum Butterfly House
Cromwell Rd, Kensington, SW7 5BD
020 7942 5511
www.nhm.ac.uk/butterflies

Whipsnade Zoo's Butterfly Paradise
The Broad Walk, NW1 4SX
020 7449 6200
www.zsl.org/butterfly-house

CASTLES & HOUSES

Chiswick House and Gardens
Burlington Lane, Chiswick, W4 2RP
020 3141 3350
www.chiswickhouseandgardens.org.uk

Down House
Luxted Road, Downe, Orpington, BR6 7JT
www.english-heritage.org.uk/visit/places/
home-of-charles-darwin-down-house
01689 859 119

Fenton House and Garden
Hampstead Grove, Hampstead, NW3 6SP
020 7435 3471
www.nationaltrust.org.uk/fenton-house-
and-garden

Hall Place and Gardens
Bourne Road, Bexley,
DA5 1PQ
01322 526 574
www.hallplace.org.uk

Kenwood House

Hampstead Lane, Highgate, NW3 7JR
0370 333 1181
www.english-heritage.org.uk/visit/places/
kenwood

Osterley Park and House

Jersey Road, Isleworth, TW7 4RB
020 8232 5050
www.nationaltrust.org.uk/osterley-park-
and-house

Palm House, Royal Botanic Gardens

Kew, Richmond, TW9 3EF
020 8332 5655
www.kew.org

Severndroog Castle

Castle Wood, Shooters Hill, SE18 3RT
0800 689 1796
www.severndroogcastle.org.uk

CITY FARMS

Deen City Farm

39 Windsor Ave, SW19 2RR
020 8543 5300
www.deencityfarm.co.uk

Kentish Town City Farm

1 Cressfield Close, NW5 4BN
020 7916 5421
www.ktcityfarm.org.uk

Lee Valley Park Farms

Stubbins Hall Lane, Waltham Abbey,
EN9 2EF
01992 892 781
www.lvfarms.co.uk

Mudchute Park and Farm

Pier Street, Isle of Dogs, E14 3HP
020 7515 5901
www.mudchute.org

Oasis Waterloo Farm

1A Kennington Rd, Lambeth, SE1 7QP
020 7921 4242
www.oasiswaterloo.org/farm

Stepney City Farm
Stepney Way, E1 3DG
020 7790 8204
www.stepneycityfarm.org

Woodlands Farm
331 Shooters Hill, Welling, DA16 3RP
020 8319 8900
www.woodlandsfarmtrust.org

CYCLING

Alexandra Palace
Alexandra Palace Way, N22 7AY
020 8365 2121
www.alexandrapalace.com

Chelsea Physic Garden
Curators House, 66 Royal Hospital Road,
SW3 4HS
020 7352 5646
www.chelseaphysicgarden.co.uk

Ham House and Gardens
Ham Street, Richmond-upon-Thames,
TW10 7RS
020 8940 1950
www.nationaltrust.org.uk/ham-house-and-garden

Highgate Wood
Muswell Hill Road, Highgate, N10 3JN
020 8444 6129
www.cityoflondon.gov.uk/things-to-do/green-spaces/highgate-wood

Isabella Plantation
Richmond Park, Kingston upon Thames,
KT2 7NA
0300 061 2200
www.royalparks.org.uk/parks/richmond-park/isabella-plantation

Kyoto Garden
Holland Park, Holland Park Avenue,
Kensington, W11 4UA
020 7361 3003
www.parkgrandkensington.co.uk

Morden Hall Park
Morden Hall Road, SM4 5JD
020 8545 6850
www.nationaltrust.org.uk
/morden-hall-park

Pembroke Lodge
Richmond Park, Queen Street,
Richmond, TW10 5HX
020 8940 8207
www.pembroke-lodge.co.uk

Queen Elizabeth Olympic Park
Stratford, E20 2ST

Rosmead Gardens
Rosmead Road, W11 2JG

Springfield Park
61 Ashtead Rd, E5 9BL
020 8356 3000
www.hackney.gov.uk/springfield-park

Tottenham Marshes
Watermead Way, N17 0XD
0300 003 0610
www.visitleevalley.org.uk

ECO PARKS

Camley Street Nature Park
12 Camley Street, N1C 4PW
020 3897 6150
www.wildlondon.org.uk/reserves/
camley-street-natural-park

Gillespie Park
10 Tannington Terrace, Gillespie Rd,
N5 1LE
020 7527 4374
www.friendsofgillespiepark.co.uk

Greenwich Peninsula Ecology Park
The Ecology Park Gatehouse, SE10 0QZ
020 8293 1904
greenwichpeninsulawildlifeheritage.co.uk

ORGANISATIONS

Bees, Wasps and Ants Recording Society
www.bwars.com

BioBlitz
www.bnhc.org.uk/bioblitz

Bumblebee Conservation Trust
www.bumblebeeconservation.org

The Conservation Volunteers
www.tcv.org.uk

Earthworm Society of Britain
www.earthwormsoc.org.uk

FoodCycle
www.foodcycle.org.uk

Good Gym
www.goodgym.org

Green Gym
www.tcv.org.uk/greengym

London Bat Group
londonbats.org.uk

The London Wildlife Trust
www.wildlondon.org.uk

RSPB
www.rspb.org.uk

Sustrans
www.sustrans.org.uk

Thames 21
www.thames21.org.uk

Woodland Trust
www.woodlandtrust.org.uk

PICK-YOUR-OWN

Copas Farm
Calves Lane Farm, Billet Lane, Iver,
SL0 0LU
01753 652 727
www.copasfarms.co.uk

Garsons Farm
Winterdown Road, West End, Esher, Surrey,
KT10 8LS
01372 464 389
www.garsons.co.uk

Parkside Farm
Hadley Road, Enfield, EN2 8LA
020 8367 2035
www.parksidefarmpyo.co.uk

SECRET GARDENS

Abney Park
Stoke Newington Church Street,
N16 1AU
020 7275 7557
www.abneypark.org

Bonnington Square Pleasure Gardens
11C Bonnington Square, SW8 1TE
020 7450 3773
www.bonningtonsquaregarden.org.uk

Geffrye Museum Garden
136 Kingsland Road, E2 8EA
020 7739 9893
www.geffrye-museum.org.uk

King Henry's Walk Garden
11c King Henry's Walk, N1 4NX
020 7923 9035
www.khwgarden.org.uk

Phoenix Garden
21 Stacey Street, WC2H 8DG
www.thephoenixgarden.org

Queen Elizabeth Hall Roof Garden
Southbank Centre, Belvedere Road,
SE1 8XX
www.southbankcentre.co.uk

Red Cross Garden
50 Redcross Way, SE1 1HA
020 7403 3393
www.london-se1.co.uk/places/red-cross-garden

St-Dunstan-in-the-East
St Dunstan's Hill, EC3R 5DD
020 7374 4127
www.cityoflondon.gov.uk/things-to-do/green-spaces/city-gardens/visitor-information/Pages/St-Dunstan-in-the-East

Centre for Wildlife Gardening
28 Marsden Road, SE15 4EE
020 3897 6151
www.wildlondon.org.uk/reserves/centre-for-wildlife-gardening

SWIMMING

Brockwell Lido
Brockwell Park, Dulwich Road,
SE24 0PA
020 7274 3088
www.fusion-lifestyle.com/centres/
brockwell-lido

Charlton Lido
Hornfair Park, Shooters Hill Road,
SE18 4LX
020 8856 7389
www.better.org.uk/leisure-centre/london/
greenwich/charlton-lido

Kenwood Ladies' Pond
Highgate, N6 6HQ
www.klpa.org.uk

London Fields Lido
London Fields West Side, E8 3EU
020 7254 9038
www.better.org.uk/leisure-centre/london/
hackney/london-fields-lido

Serpentine Lido
Hyde Park, South Carriage Drive, W2 2UH
020 7706 3422
serpentineswimmingclub.com

Tooting Bec Lido
Tooting Bec Road, SW16 1RU
020 8871 7198
www.placesforpeopleleisure.org/centres/
tooting-bec-lido

WATER SPORTS

Almost Wild Campsite
Nazeing New Road, Broxbourne,
Hertfordshire, EN10 6TD
0300 003 0632
www.visitleevalley.org.uk

Brent Reservoir
Hendon, NW9 7ND
www.canalrivertrust.org.uk/places-to-visit/
brent-reservoir-welsh-harp

Farncombe Boat House
Catteshall Road, Godalming, GU7 1NH
01483 421 306
www.farncombeboats.co.uk

Frensham Great Pond
Farnham, GU10 3DX

Shadwell Basin Outdoor Activity Centre
3–4 Shadwell Pierhead, Glamis Road,
E1W 3TD
020 7481 4210
www.shadwell-basin.co.uk

Tamesis Club
Trowlock Way, Teddington, TW11 9QY
020 8977 3589
www.tamesisclub.co.uk

West Reservoir Centre
Green Lanes, Hackney, N4 2HA
020 8442 8116
www.better.org.uk/leisure-centre/london/
hackney/west-reservoir-centre

WILDLIFE SANCTUARIES

Braeburn Park
Lower Station Road, Crayford, DA1 3RG
020 7261 0447
www.wildlondon.org.uk/reserves/braeburn-
park

**Crane Meadows (or Huckerby's
Meadows)**
Waye Avenue, Cranford, TW5 9SH
020 3897 6153
www.wildlondon.org.uk/reserves/
huckerbys-meadows

London Wetland Centre
Queen Elizabeth's Walk, Barnes,
SW13 9WT

Walthamstow Wetlands
2 Forest Road, N17 9NH
020 8496 2115
www.walthamstowwetlands.com

NOTES

Barton, J., R. Bragg, J., Pretty, M. Rogerson, 'The health and wellbeing impacts of volunteering with The Wildlife Trusts,' University of Essex, 2017

Byrd-McDevitt, Lori, 'The 10 Coolest Musems', *The New York Times*, 30 Jan 2018

Gill, Tim, *No Fear* (Calouste Gulbenkian Foundation, 2007)

Harari, Yuval Noah, *Sapiens* (Harvill Secker, 2011)

Heaney, Seamus, 'Blackberry-Picking', *Death of a Naturalist* (Faber & Faber Poetry, 1966)

Moore, Rowan, 'Garden Museum review', *Guardian*, 28 May 2017

INDEX

Abney Park, 31, 135
Abundance London, 107
acorns, 118
Age UK, 48
agrimony, 25
air pollution, 3, 25
Alara Wholefoods, 114
alder trees, 126
Alexandra Palace, 43, 79, 81, 168
Almost Wild, 66
amphibians, 12
ancient bye-laws, 73
Ancient Tree Hunt, 98
ancient woodland, 95–103
apples, apple trees, 13, 86, 103, 113, *115*, 134
apricots, 113, 114
arboreta, 31
Archway Road, 81
Arsenal FC, 15, 29
ash trees, 32, 99, 126
Attenborough, David, 98, 140
Aulis, 149
autumn colours, 126–8
avocets, 134
azaleas, 22–4, *23*, 78

Balham Farmers' Market, 43
Ball's Pond, 31
Bankside, 37
Barbican, 154–6
Barley Mow pub, Tilford, 57

barley, 26
Barn Elms, 140
Barnes Wetland Centre, *132*
Barnes, 63
Barrie, James Matthew, 164
Bates, Herbert Ernest, *95*
bats, 81, 87–9, 137, 143
Battersea, x, 149
Battersea Park, 98, 124
Battersea Power Station, 78, 92, 141
beachcombing, 60
bears, 101
Beckton, 63
beech trees, 99, 100, 124, 126
Bees, Wasps and Ants Recording Society
(BWARS), 51
bees, x, 10, 13, 15, 25, 27, 32, 34, *50*, 51, 99, 114,
137, 162
beetles, 25
BeeWatchers, 51
Belsize Park, 165
Berkeley Plane, 121
Berkeley Square, 121
berries, 105–11, 133
Bethlem Royal Hospital, 113
Bexley, *156*
Big Ben, 138
Big Butterfly Count, 10
Big Clean-Up, The, 49
Big Garden Birdwatch, 51
Billingsgate Fish Market, 86

bindweed, 37
BioBlitz, 51
Biodiversity Action Teams (BATs), 49
Biodiversity Partnership, 160
biodiversity, 25
bird tables, 48, 87
birds, 49, 51, 70, 86, 133–44
    avocets, 134
    bitterns, 141
    blackbirds, 36, 134
    blackcaps, 135
    blue tits, 36
    buzzards, 19, 135
    Cetti's warblers, 134
    chiffchaffs, 134
    coots, 70, 134, 156
    cormorants, 144
    ducks, x, 141
    firecrests, 137
    goldcrests, 134, 137
    goldfinches, 155
    great tits, 36
    grebes, 156
    greenfinches, 36
    herons, 70, 134
    hobbies, 19
    hole-nesting, 97
    house martins, 86
    kestrels, 19, 36, 135
    kingfishers, 15, 19, 56, 70, 134, 140
    kites, 19, 135
    lapwings, 134
    marsh harriers, 134
    merlins, 135
    moorhens, 134
    nuthatches, 19, 56, 137
    owls, 72, 134, 135, 137, *151*
    parakeets, 78, 86–7
    pelicans, 134
    peregrine falcons, 92–3, 141
    pied flycatchers, 97
    plovers, 134, 140
    redstarts, 97
    robins, 36, 133, 134
    song thrushes, 118, 134
    sparrowhawks, 36, 135
    sparrows, 134
    starlings, 138
    swallows, 86
    swans, 134
    swifts, 143
    terns, 86
    treecreepers, 103
    waders, 134
    warblers, x, 13, 86
    water birds, 134
    waxwings, 133
    wigeons, 141
    woodpeckers, 19, 36, 70, 97, 135
    wrens, 13, 36, 134, 137
Bishopsgate, 113
bitterns, 141
blackberries, 105–11
blackbirds, 36, 134
Blackbush Wood, 98–9
blackcaps, 135
Blackfriars Bridge, 63
Blackheath, 167
Bleak House (Dickens), 147
Blitz (1940–41), 30, 37, 54

blue tits, 36
bluebells, *16*, 17–19, 97
Bonnington Square, 37–9, *38*
Boogaloo pub, 81
boot camps, 43, *47*
Boris bikes, 69
Borough Market, 45
Boxing Day, 134, 165
Braeburn Park, 3
Brent Reservoir, 66
Brentford, 63
Brighton, 69
British Nutrition Foundation, 106
British Wildlife Photography Awards, 152
Brixton Farmers' Market, 43
Brockley Farmers' Market, 43
Brockwell Lido, 54
Bromley, 87, 98, 113, 118
Brompton, 135, 137
brownfield sites, x
Broxbourne, Hertfordshire, 66
Brutalism, 154–5
BT Tower, 140
Buckingham Palace Gardens, 29
buddleia, 37
bug hotels, 32, 48
Bumblebee Conservation Trust, 51
bumblebees, 27, 99
Bushy Park, 90
buttercups, 25
butterflies, 9–10, 13, 25, 51, 99, 137
buzzards, 19, 135
Byron, George Gordon, 101
caddis flies, 89
Callander, Jane, 20

Cambridgeshire, 45
Camden Lock, 167
camellias, 19–20
Camley Street Nature Park, *11*, 13–15, *112*
canals, x, 13–15, 64, 70, 75, 134, 165, 167
Canary Wharf, 7, 64
candytuft, 36
Cannizaro Park, 22
canoeing, *53*, 56, 64–6, 110
canuting, 64
Cape Wrath, 18
carrier pigeons, 92
Cavendish, William, 6th Duke of Devonshire, 19
cemeteries, 31, *50*, 73, 135–7, *136*
Centre for Wildlife Gardening, *32*, 33
Cetti's warblers, 134
Chalet Wood, 18
Chalk Farm, 165
Chandler, Alfred, 19
Channel Tunnel, 110
Charing Cross Hospital, 93
Charles II, King of England, Scotland and Ireland, 30, 53, 122
Charles VI, Holy Roman Emperor, 117
Charles, Prince of Wales, 27
Charlton Lido, 54
Chase Nature Reserve, 86
Château King's Cross, 114
Chaucer, Geoffrey, 117
Chelsea, 98, 149
Chelsea College of Art, 72
Chelsea Flower Show, 26, 33
Chelsea Physic Garden, 73–5
chequers berries, 101
cherries, cherry trees, 113, 114, 126

Chessington Zoo, 45
chiffchaffs, 134
children's farm movement, 4
Chiswick, 107
Chiswick House, 19–20
Chiswick Pier, 63
Christmas, 113, 159–68
churches, 30
Cincinnati Zoo, 151
City Airport, 57
city farms, 3, 4–9, 70, 72, 167
City Hall, 98
City of London, 156
Claudius Roman Emperor, 117
Clissold Park, 21, 104, 120, 124, 158, 168
clover, 25
Colliers Wood, 70
Collins, Marilyn, 79
Columbia Creative, 160
Columbia Road Flower Market, 160
common spotted orchid, 15
conifer trees, 100
Conker Tree Science, 123
conkers, 123, 125
conservation, 3, 25, 45, 46, 48–51, 114
Cooke, Jack, 124
coots, 70, 134, 156
Copas Farm, 41, 44
Coppermill Tower, 144
Core Blimey, 113
Corkscrew, 124
cormorants, 144
Cornwall, 79, 148
Coronation Meadows project, 27
Corporation of London, 30

Covent Garden, 36, 160
cow parsley, 15
cowslips, 25
crab apples, 104
Crane Meadows, 3
Craven Cottage, 140
Crayford, 3
Critical Mass, 69
crocuses, 21–2, 21
Cromwell, Oliver, 122
Crooked Billet, 58
Crouch End Hill, 79
Crown Estate, 61
Croydon, 70
Cudham Valley, 98
cyclamen, 21
cycling, 58, 60, 69–81, 98

daffodils, 21
Dalston, 9
Dartford, 138
Darwin, Charles, 98–9
Daubenton's bat, 89
Deen City Farm, 72
deer, 81, 85, 90, 91, 117
Department of Transport, 103
Deptford, 49, 61, 63
Devonshire, Duke of, see Cavendish, William
Dickens, Charles, 54, 147
Docwra's Wood, 32
dog violet, 99
Domesday Book, 56
Dove, The, 167
Downe House, 98
Downing Street, 29

Druids, 159
Dryden, John, 117
ducks, x, 141
Dunnett, Nigel, 26, 155
Dunwich Dynamo, 69
Dutch elm disease, 15, 122

Earthly Paradise, The (Morris), ix
Earthworm Society of Britain, 51
East Lothian, 97
eco-parks, 3, 10–15
Edgware, 79
Edible City, The (Rensten), 105, 107
Edward II, King of England, 53
Effra river, 49
Eliot, George, 137
Elizabeth II Queen of the United Kingdom, 154
elm trees, 15, 122
Eltham, 114
l'Enclume, 148
Enfield, 44
Epping Forest, 12, 76, 90, *96*, 114, 116, 117
Esher, Surrey, 44–5
Essex, 58–60, *59*
Excel Centre, 57
Exmoor Bolving Competition, 90

Faesten Dic, 100
fairies, 79, 117
Fairlop Waters, 86
false acacia trees, 98
farm-to-hand, x, 43–5
farm-to-table, x, 43, 148–9
farmers' markets, 43
Farnham, Surrey, 57

Fenton House, 114, *115*
Ferry Boat Inn, 143–4
field maple trees, 126
Finsbury Park, *47*, *68*, 79
firecrests, 137
First World War (1914–18), 100
flooding, 25
flowers
    azaleas, 22–4, *23*, 78
    bluebells, *16*, 17–19, 97, 99, 100
    camellias, 19–20
    cow parsley, 15
    crocuses, 21–2, *21*
    cyclamen, 21
    daffodils, 21
    gentian, 99
    geraniums, 36
    honeysuckle, 56, 100
    irises, 37
    lady's smock, 19
    lavender, 33
    lily of the valley, 100
    marigolds, 26
    orchids, 15, 25, 98, 99
    poppies, 33
    rhododendrons, 22–4
    snowdrops, 21
    stitchwort, 19
    tickseed, 26
    townhall clock, 99
    tulips, 37
    vetches, 15, 25
    violets, 17, 99
    wild carrot, 15
    wild garlic, 19

wisteria, *xi*, 19, 39
wood anemone, 19, 97, 99
wood sage, 100
wood sorrel, 19, 99
  yellow archangel, 99
FoodCycle, 48
foraging, 104–18
Foreign Cattle Market, 61
forest gardening, 15
Forest Hill, 149
Forest School, 4
Forestry Commission, 100
Fortnum & Mason, 22
foxes, 79, 87, 99
Francis' woolly horseshoe bat, 89
Frays Farm Meadows, 89
Frazer, James, 39
Frensham Great Pond, *42*, 57
frogs, 13, 36
Fulham, 98, 110, 161
Fulham FC, 140
fungi, 97, 106, 114–17, 135
Fungi to Be With, 117

Gabriel's Wharf, 63
Garden Museum, 152
Garsons Farm, 44–5
Geffrye Museum, *xi*, 33–6, *35*
gentian, 99
geraniums, 36
Gherkin, 78
ghosts, 79, 97, 143–4
Gibbet Field, 101
Gill, Tim, 4
Gillespie Park, *14*, 15

Gladwin brothers, 149
Glingbobs, 97
goat man, 79
Godalming, Surrey, 57
goldcrests, 134, 137
goldfinches, 155
Good Gym, 46
graffiti, *33*, 75, 79, *80*
Granny Pine, 124
grasses, 25–6
grasshoppers, 25
Great Ditch Wood, 18
Great Fire of London (1666), 30
Great North Wood, 49
great spotted woodpeckers, 19
Great Storm (1987), 122
great tits, 36
grebes, 156
Green Exercise Team, 48
Green Gyms, 45–8
Green Park, 27, 29, 30
green woodpeckers, 19
greenfinches, 36
Greenwich Park, *166*, *167*, *168*
Greenwich Peninsula Ecology Park, 13
Guildford, Surrey, 57
Gurt Wurm, 97
Gutteridge Wood, 18
gyms, 45–8

Hackney, 63, 112
Hackney Harvest, 107
Hackney Marshes, 64, 109, 165
Hackney Wick, 75
Hadleigh Country Park, 60

Hall Place and Gardens, 156
Ham House and Garden, 78
Hamlet (Shakespeare), 17
Hammersmith, 110, 121
Hammersmith Bridge, 167
Hampstead Heath, 56, 89, *94*, 109, 117, 123, 134, 156, 164, 165, 168
Hampstead Observatory, 153
Hampstead, 114
Hatfeild, Gilliat Edward, 72
hawthorn trees, 56, 110, 155, 160
hazel trees, 18
Heaney, Seamus, 107
Heathrow, 3
hedgehogs, 51, 81
hedgerows, 103, 105, 109
heem parks, 10
Henry VIII, King of England and Ireland, 31, 167
herons, 70, 134
Hertfordshire, 66
hibernaculum, 32
Highbury, 29
Highbury Island, 124
Highgate, 79, 81, 135, *136*, 137, 164
Hillingdon, 18, 89
Himalayan balsam, 106
Hitchmough, James, 26
hobbies, 19
hole-nesting birds, 97
Holland Park, 73, 126
holm oak trees, 98
homeopathy, 75
honeysuckle, 56, 100
Hopkins, Gerard Manley, 18
hornbeam trees, 32, 81

Horniman Museum and Gardens, 10, 149–52
horse and harrow, 27
horse chestnut trees, 123
House and Garden Apple Weekend, 114
house martins, 86
Houses of Parliament, 93
Howgate Wonder, 112
Hoxton, 34
Hubbard, James Henry, 151
Hyde Park, 27, 56, 73, 164

Incredible Edible Lambeth Harvest, 107
irises, 37
Isabella Plantation, 24, 78
Isle of Dogs, 7
Isles of Scilly, 18
Islington, 15, *28*, 31–3, 134
Iver, Buckinghamshire, 44
ivy, 137

James, Anne, 103
Jamie's Farm, Wiltshire, 7
Japanese knotweed, 106
Jekyll, Gertrude, 152
Jericho Road Project, 161
Jones, Alun, 152
Joyden's Wood, 100–101
Judas trees, 39

kayaking, 53, 67
Keats, John, 18
Kensal Green, 135, 161
Kensington, 110
Kent, 101, 161
Kentish Town City Farm, 4, 5

Kenwood House, *23*, 24
Kenwood Ladies' Pond, 56
kestrels, 19, 36, 135
Kew Bridge, 63
Kew Gardens, 22, 98, 126, *129*, 156, 162, *163*
kidney vetch, 15
King Alfred's cake, 66
King Henry's Mound, 78, 168
King Henry's Walk Garden, *28*, 31–3
King, Stephen, 79
King's Christmas Trees, 161
King's Cross, *11*, 13–15, 49, 114
kingfishers, 15, 19, *56*, 70, 134, 140
Kingsland Road, 34
Kingston Bridge, 67
kites, 19, 135
kitesurfing, 58
knapweed, 25
knot gardens, 34
Kraken, The, 124
Kyoto Garden, 73, 126

lacewings, 33
Ladbroke Grove, 72
lady's smock, 19
ladybirds, 33
Lake District, 148
Lambeth, 49, 152
lapwings, 134, 140
lavender, 33
Laycock Street Park, 134
Lea river, 64, 66, 75, 118, 143–4, 165
Lea Rowing Club, 75
Lea Valley, 107, 134, 143
Lea Valley Road, 76

leaf miner moth, 123
Lee Valley Farms, *2*, *5*, 109
Leicester Square, 138
Leigh-on-Sea, Essex, 58–60, *59*
lemon slugs, 97
Lewisham, 167
lichen, 15
lidos, 53, 54, *55*
light pollution, 64, 89, 153
lily of the valley, 100
Limehouse, 64
Linear Park, 156–7
Linnaeus, Carl, 22
Litter Heroes, 49
Little Wormwood Scrubs, 134
Littlebrook Power Station, 138
Litvinenko, Alexander, 137
Lockwood, 143
London Bat Group, 89
London Bridge, 30, 54
London Fields Lido, 54, *55*
London Mudlark, 63
London Orchard Festival, 113
London Stadium, 168
London Wetland Centre, 140–41, 167
London Wildlife Trust (LWT), 3, 13, 49, 51
London Zoo, 10, 162
Lordship Lane, 149
Lost Effra project, 49
Love's Labour's Lost (Shakespeare), 34
Lucas Gardens, 124
lynx, 100

Mabey, Richard, x
Maiklem, Lara, 63

Malone, Kate, 34
mangalitsa pigs, 148
Manor Park, 76
Marchington, James, 86–7
marigolds, 26
marsh harriers, 134
marsh samphire, 58
Marx, Karl, 137
Marylebone, 148–9
Marylebone Elm, 122
Marylebone Farmers' Market, 43
Master's Garden, 29
maypoles, 37
medlars, 113
Men in Sheds, 48
mental health, 7, 27, 46, 48, 114
merlins, 135
Merton Abbey Mills, 70
Merton Joy, 112
mice, 85
Mildmay, 33
Mill Hill Park, 114
Millennium Bridge, 63
MIND, 46, 114
mini-beast hunting, 12, 33, 66
Ministry of Defence, 137
mistletoe, 159–60
moles, 117
MoMA, New York, 149
monkshood, 34
Monterey Pine, 124
Moon Phase Survey, 89
moorhens, 134
Morden Hall Park, 71, 72
Morris, William, ix

Morrison, David, 92
moths, 123, 137
Mudchute Park and Farm, 5–7, 6
mudlarking, 60–63, 62
mugwort, x, 118
muntjac deer, 81
museums, 149–53
    Garden Museum, 152–3
    Geffrye Museum, xi, 33–6, 35
    Horniman Museum and Gardens, 10, 149–52
    Natural History Museum, 8, 9, 54, 89
    OrganicLea Vestry House Museum, 107
mushrooms, 114–17
Muswell Hill, 81

National Gardens Scheme, 73
National Health Service (NHS), 46, 48
National Meadows Day, 27
National Trust, 37
Natural England, 103
Natural History Museum, 8, 9, 54, 89
naturalists, 51
Nature and Wellbeing Act, 3
nature reserves, 3
nature walks, 48
Netherlands, 4, 10
nettles, 118
Newington Green, 31
newts, 12, 100–101, 103
Nine Elms, 36, 156
noctule bat, 89
Noma, 106
Norfolk Broads, 140
Northamptonshire, 123
Notting Hill, 72, 149

nudism, 56, 69
Nunhead, *50*, 135
Nutbourne, 149
nuthatches, 19, 56, 137

oak trees, 18, 81, 98, 100, 118, 122, 128
Oasis Waterloo, 7
oBikes, 69
Observatory of University College London, 153
Octavia Hill, 37
Old Ship, 167
Olympic Games, 26, *56*, 60
Olympic Park, 26, 75, 165, 168
One Fine Tree, 161
Open Gardens Squares Weekend, 29, 73
orchards, 103, 112–14
orchids, 15, 25, 98, 99
OrganicLea Vestry House Museum, 107
Orpington, 101
Osborne Bros, 58
Osterley Park, 19, 129
otters, 85
outdoor gyms, 45–8
Overall, Andy, 116–17
owls, 72, 134, 135, 137, *151*
Oxleas Wood, 19, 101–3, *102*
OXO Tower, 93
oxygen, 19, 54, 60, 85
oysters, 58, 61

Paddington Old Cemetery, 124
Paddle & Pick, 63
paddleboarding, 63
palmate newts, 103
Paradise Project, 39

parakeets, 78, 86–7
Parkland Walk, 79–81, *80*
Parkside Farm, 44
Parliament Hill, 43, 165, 168
Partridges, 22
pears, 103, 113
Pearson, Dan, 39
Peckham, *32*, 33
pelargonium pyramids, 36
pelicans, 134
Peltigera didactyla, 15
Pembroke Lodge, 78, 168
Pepys, Samuel, 101
Père Lachaise cemetery, 135
peregrine falcons, 92–3, 103, 141
pergola, 34, 36, 39
PETA (People for the Ethical Treatment of Animals), 87
Peter Pan Cup, 164
Petersham Nurseries, 78, 160
Phantom Squad, 78
Phoenix, The, 168
Phoenix Garden, 36–7
pick-your-own farms, 43–5
pied flycatchers, 97
Pimlico Road Farmers' Market, 43
pipistrelle bats, 87–9
Pitt Cue, 148
PlantTracker, 51
plovers, 134, 140
plums, 103
pochard ducks, 141
pollution, 3, 25, 64, 89, 121
ponds, 10
    Ball's Pond, 31

Barbican Conservatory, 155–6
Centre for Wildlife Gardening, 33
eco-parks, 12
Frensham Great Pond, *42*, 57
Hampstead Heath, 56, 109, 164
Isabella Plantation, 24
Joyden's Wood, 100
Kenwood Ladies' Pond, 56
King Henry's Walk Garden, 32
Kyoto Garden, 126
London Wetland Centre, 143
Oxleas Wood, 103
Red Cross Garden, 37
West Reservoir Centre, 66
Whitestone Pond, 153
Pool of London, 60
Pope, Alexander, 117
poppies, 33
porpoises, 86
Port of London, 61
potsherds, 61
Potter, Beatrix, 107
Pressmennan Wood, 97
Primrose Hill, *83*, *125*, *127*, 165
Priory Lane, 57
Prittle Brook, 58
Pulbrook & Gould, 160
Putney Bridge, 167
Puttenham Common, 117
pygmy shrew, 89

Queen Elizabeth Hall Roof Garden, 27
Queen Elizabeth Olympic Park, 26, 75, 165, 168
quinces, 113

Rabbit, 149
railway tracks, x, 15, 70, 79, 109
Rainham Marshes, 134, 137–40, *139*
Rape of Lucrece, The (Shakespeare), 92
Ravenscourt Park, 121
Red Cross Garden, 37
red kites, 19, 135
red oak, 128
Redzepi, René, 106
Regent's Canal, 13, 64
Regent's Park, 30, *108*, 167
Rensten, John, *104*, 107
rhododendrons, 22–4
Richmond, 54, 160
Richmond Park, 24, 76–8, 77, 90, *91*, 168
Richmond Royal Oak, 122
RideLondon, 69
ringed plovers, 134
roadside verges, x
robins, 36, 133, 134
Rogan, Simon, 148–9
Romanticism, 18
rooftop farms, 9
rooftop gardens, 39
Rosmead Gardens, 72–3
Rotherhithe, 64
Royal Docks, 57
Royal Maritime Museum, 167
Royal Oaks, 122
Royal Observatory, 167, 168
Royal Parks, 27, 73, 134
Royal Society for the Protection of Birds (RSPB),
49, 51, 87, 137–40
Russell, Bertrand, 78
Rutherford, Margaret, 54

Ryan, Rob, 33
Rye Meads, 137, 140

Sabin, Andrew, 72
Saffron Walden, 22, 58–60
saffron, 22
sailing, 66–7
Santander Cycles, 69, 72
Santolina chamaecyparissus, 34
Save our Magnificent Meadows, 27
Savernake Forest, 97
Sawyer's Hill, 78
Scadbury Acorn Trail, 118
school farms, 4
Scilly Isles, 18
Scotland, 18, 97, 124
Scott, Peter, 140
sea beet, 106
seahorses, 86
seals, 86
Second World War (1939–45), 20, 25, 30, 37, 54, 78, 92, 100, 116
Secret Adventures, 64
sedum, 72
Selfridges, 151
Selhurst, 49
Serpentine Swimming Club, 56, 164
Severndroog Castle, 19, *102*, 103
sewers, 49, 54
Shadwell Basin, 66–7, 67
Shakespeare, William, 17, 34, 92
Shalford Park, 57
Shard, 78
Shed, The, 149
sheep, 27

Shepperton Studios, 86
Shervage Wood, 97
Sherwood Forest, 97
Shoebury East Beach, 58
Shooter's Hill, 19, 101
Shropshire, 122
silver birch trees, 32, 100
Silver Jubilee Walkway, 12
Silverstone, 57
Site of Special Scientific Interest, 19, 66, 76
Sites of Importance for Nature Conservation, 135
Sky Garden, 156
sledging, x, 167
Sleyt, The, 24
Slimbridge Wetlands, 140
slugs, 97
Snowdon Aviary, 167
snowdrops, 21
social prescribing, 48
Soho, 148, 149
Somerset, 97
song thrushes, 118, 134
South Acton, 114
South Bank, 63, 148
South London Christmas Trees, 161
Southbank Centre, 27
Southend-on-Sea, Essex, 58
Southwark, 37
Southwark Bridge, 63
sparrowhawks, 36, 135
sparrows, 134
Special Area of Conservation, 76
Spencer, Stanley, 54
spotted orchids, 25

spriggan, 79
Springfield Park, 75
squirrels, *84*, 85, 123
St Andrew's Church, Totteridge, 121
St Dunstan-in-the-East, *1*, 30
St Giles-in-the-Fields, 36
St James's Palace, 30
St John's Church, 161
St Pancras station, 13, 114
St Paul's Cathedral, *63*, 78, *93*, 168
St Paul's Church, Stoke Newington, 161
St-Mary-at-Lambeth church, 152
stag beetles, 13
stargazing, 153–4
starlings, 138
Stephens, Henry Charles 'Inky', 15
Stephenson, George, 152
Stepney City Farm, 7
stitchwort, 19
Stoke Newington, 31, 66, 134, 161
strawberry trees, 98
street art, 33, *75*, 79, *80*
Suffolk, 69, 81
sunflowers, 72
Surrey, 12, 44–5, *56–7*, 110
Sustrans, 48
Swain's Lane, 137
swallows, 86
swans, 134
sweet chestnut trees, 98, 100
swifts, 143
swimming spots, x, *52*, 53–60, 64, 66, 164
    Brockwell Lido, 54
    Charlton Lido, 54
    Frensham Great Pond, *42*, 57

Hampstead Heath, 56, 109, 164
Kenwood Ladies' Pond, 56
Leigh-on-Sea, 58
London Fields Lido, 54, *55*
Royal Docks, 57
Serpentine Swimming Club, 56
Thames Baths Lido, 54
Tideswell, *52*
Tooting Bec Lido, 54
West Reservoir Centre, 66
Wey river, 56–7
sycamore trees, 32, 98
Sydenham Hill Wood, *88*, 89

Tamesis Club, 67
Tamsin Trail, 76–8
Tate Modern, 63, *93*
tawny owls, 134, 135, 137
TCV (The Conservation Volunteers), 46, 49
Teddington, 60, 67
Temple, 18, 29
Tennyson, Alfred, 18, 117
terns, 86
terrapins, 103, 156
Thames Baths Lido, 54
Thames Clipper, 64
Thames Estuary, 60
Thames Gateway, 60, 137
Thames river, ix, 12, 27, 53–4, 60–64, 85–6, 134
    as biologically dead, 54, 85
    canoeing, 64
    commuting, 64
    conservation, 49, 54, 63, 85
    kitesurfing, 58
    London Wetland Centre, 140

mudlarking, 60–63, *62*
paddleboarding, *63*
Rainham Marshes, 138
sailing, 66–7
Shoebury East Beach, 58
swimming in, 53–4
TideFest, 63
Tideway, 60
wildlife, 85–6, 134
Thames21, 49
tickseed, 26
TideFest, 63
Tideswell, *52*
Tideway, 60
tiger butterflies, *8*
Tilford, Surrey, *56*
Tootflits, 97
Tooting Bec Lido, 54
Tottenham, 12, 143
Tottenham Marshes, 76
Totteridge, 121
Tower Bridge, 12, 64
Tower Hamlets, 135, 137
Tower of London, 30, 73
townhall clock, 99
Tradescant, John, 152
Treasure Act (1996), 61–3
Tree Climber's Guide, The (Cooke), 124
Tree Council, 122
Tree of Heaven, 121
treecreepers, 103
trees, 98, 121–9
    apple, 13, 86, 103, 113, 134
    ash, 32, 99, 126
    beech, 99, 100, 124, 126

    cherry, 113, 114, 126
    conifers, 100
    elm, 15, 122
    false acacias, 98
    field maple, 126
    hawthorn, 56, 110, 155, 160
    hazel, 18
    holm oak, 98
    hornbeam, 32, 81
    horse chestnut, 123
    Judas, 39
    oak, 18, 81, 98, 100, 118, 122, 126, 128
    silver birch, 32, 100
    strawberry, 98
    sycamore, 32, 98
    sweet chestnut, 98, 100
    walnut, 37
    yew, 121
Trent Country Park, 44
tulips, 37
Tweed Run, 69
Twenty Acre Shaw Wood, 98–9
Two Tree Island, 58

umami, 118
UNESCO (United Nations Educational, Scientific and Cultural Organization), 99
United States embassy, 156
University of Essex, 48
University of Greenwich, 114
urban farms, *see* city farms
Urban Orchard Project, 112, 113
Urban Urchins, 51
Van Heyningen and Haward Architects, 138
Vanguard Beech, 124

Vass technique, 32
Vauxhall Pleasure Gardens, 39
vegetable gardens, 27, 33, 43
vetches, 15, 25
Viaduct Road, 110
Victoria Lodge, 73
Victoria, Queen of the United Kingdom, 81
Victorian period (1837–1901), 9, 13, 24, 33, 36, 54, 66, 86, 112, 122, 140, 143–4, 151
vineyards, 114
violets, 17, 99
voles, 86

waders, 134
'Walkie-Talkie' tower, 156
wall germander, 34
Wallace, Alfred Russel, 9
walnut trees, 37
Walpole, Horace, 129
Waltham Forest, 49
Walthamstow Farmers' Market, 43
Walthamstow Marshes, x, 117, 118
Walthamstow Wetlands, 3, 76, 134, *142*, 143–4, *145*
Wandle Trail, 70–72
Wandsworth, 70
Wanstead Park, 18, 89
Wapping, 64
warblers, x, 13, 86
Warwick Avenue, 167
wassailing, 113
water birds, 134
water polo, 66
waterwheels, 70
waxwings, 133

weeds, 26
West Carriage Drive, 27
West Norwood, 135
West Reservoir Centre, 66
Westminster, 98
Wey river, 56–7, 110
wheat, 26
Whipsnade Zoo, 10
Whipsnade, 162
whitebeam, 32
Whitestone Pond, 153
wigeons, 141
wild carrot, 15
wildflowers, 13, 15, 25–7, *26*, 31, 99
    bluebells, *16*, 17–19, 97, 99, 100
    buttercups, 25
    cow parsley, 15
    gentian, 99
    honeysuckle, 100
    lady's smock, 19
    lily of the valley, 100
    marigolds, 26
    orchids, 15, 25, 98, 99
    stitchwort, 19
    tickseed, 26
    townhall clock, 99
    vetches, 15, 25
    violets, 17, 99
    wild carrot, 15
    wild garlic, 19
    wood anemone, 19, 97, 99
    wood sage, 100
    wood sorrel, 19, 99
    yellow archangel, 99
wild garlic, 19, 149

Wild Lights night, 162
wild nettles, 118
wildfowl, 140
Wildfowl & Wetlands Trust (WWT), 140, 141
wildlife, 85–93
    bats, 81, 87–9, 137, 143
    bees, x, 10, 13, 15, 25, 27, 32, 34, 50, 51, 99, 114, 137
    birds, *see under* birds
    butterflies, 9–10, 13, 25, 51, 99, 137
    deer, 81, 85, 90, *91*, 117
    foxes, 79, 87, 99
    frogs, 13, 36
    lemon slugs, 97
    mice, 85
    muntjac deer, 81
    newts, 12, 100–101, 103
    otters, 85
    peregrine falcons, 92–3, 103
    porpoises, 86
    seahorses, 86
    seals, 86
    squirrels, *84*, 85, 123
    voles, 86
wildlife sanctuaries, 3
Wildlife Trust, 33
Willesden, 12
William Curtis Ecological Park, 12
Willow Farm, Cambridgeshire, 45
Wimbledon, 22, 70, 110
Wimbledon Common, 117
Windsor Great Park, 20
windsurfing, 53
wine, 114
wisteria, *xi*, 19, 39

wolf's bane, 34
wolves, 101
wood anemone, 19, *97*, 99
wood sage, 100
wood sorrel, 19, 99
Woodberry Wetlands, *viii*, 134
Woodland Trust, 122
Woodlands Farms, 103
woodlands, 94–103
    Blackbush Wood, 98–9
    Epping Forest, 12, 76, 90, 96, 114, 116, 117
    Hampstead Heath, *56*, 89, *94*, 109, 117, 123, 164
    Joyden's Wood, 100–101
    Oxleas Wood, 19, 101–3, *102*
    Shooter's Hill, 19, 101
    Twenty Acre Shaw Wood, 98–9
woodpeckers, 19, 36, 70, 97, 135
World Conker Championships, 123
World Naked Bike Ride, 69
World Wide Fund for Nature (WWF), 140
Wormwood Scrubs, 110, 134
Wren, Christopher, 30
wrens, 13, 36, 134, 137

yarrow, 118
yellow archangel, 99
yellow rattle, 25
yew trees, 121

Zoological Society of London, 162

Sam and Sophie Hodges are Londoners working in film and theatre.

They have two children.